T H E   B O O K   O F

PIZZAS
& ITALIAN BREADS

T H E   B O O K   O F

PIZZAS
& ITALIAN BREADS

SARAH BUSH

Photography by
Jon Stewart,
assisted by Alister Thorpe

HPBooks
a division of
PRICE STERN SLOAN

ANOTHER BEST SELLING VOLUME FROM HPBOOKS

Published by HPBooks
A division of Price Stern Sloan, Inc.
11150 Olympic Boulevard, Suite 650
Los Angeles, CA 90064

10 9 8 7 6 5 4

By arrangement with Salamander Books Ltd. and Merehurst Press, London.

This book was created by Merehurst Limited
Ferry House, 51-57 Lacy Road, Putney, London SW15

Designer: Roger Daniels
Home Economist: Sarah Bush
Photographer: Jon Stewart, assisted by Alister Thorpe
Color separation: Kentscan Limited
Printed in Belgium by Proost Internationl Book Production

Library of Congress Cataloging-in-Publication Data

Bush, Sarah.
    The book of pizzas & Italian breads / Bush, Sarah.
      p.   cm.
    Includes Index.
    1. Salads   I. Title.
TX770.P58R63 1988   641.8'24—dc 19   88-21324
ISBN0-89586-788-5 (pbk.)

CONTENTS

INTRODUCTION

Pizza can be found in practically every country of the world. They have, in the last 10 to 15 years, become one of the mainstays of convenience and fast food eating, with pizza restaurants almost everywhere. A wide selection of fresh and frozen pizzas ready for cooking at home are also widely available from supermarkets.

From humble beginnings in the streets of Naples, the pizza has risen to become a sophisticated way to eat a wealth of delicious ingredients from simple cheese and tomato pizza, with fresh herbs and olive oil, to pizzas with exotic shellfish, oriental vegetables and spices.

It may be imagined that making pizza at home is a difficult task, but it isn't. True, the very best results are achieved by cooking them in the traditional brick ovens. However, few of us will have that luxury at home and excellent results can be produced from your own oven, and with very little effort. Don't be put off by making a yeast dough—you will soon learn that it is just as easy as making pastry. You will also find that there are several delicious alternative pizza crusts to choose from—whole-wheat, crumble-crusts, corn-meal and so on.

Pizza need not be just a snack or quick-cooked meal. They can become tempting appetizers, substantial main dishes—and even desserts—as you will see from the following pages. Included in the selection are ever-popular traditional recipes, deliciously quick and easy ideas and pizzas designed especially for children. There is also a tempting range of pizzas to serve when entertaining, plus many international ideas—and finally an interesting selection of Italian breads to choose from.

Remember that the pizza has an elegant history and has been eaten by many a king or queen—so treat it with respect. It deserves your finest ingredients. Hopefully, with the help of *The Book of Pizzas & Italian Breads,* with over 100 easy-to-follow recipes, each illustrated with a beautiful color picture, you will discover a world of pizzas just waiting to be tasted.

THE HISTORY OF PIZZAS

In Naples one summer, around the late 1800s, Queen Margherita of Savoy was residing with her family in Capodimonte Park. She had heard a lot about pizza and decided to try it for herself. The local pizza maker was summoned and he served her a pizza with a newly invented topping. From then on, the tomato, mozzarella cheese and fresh basil pizza has been known as Pizza Margherita.

Until this time, pizza had been sold in the streets to people at breakfast, lunch and dinner. It was cut from a large tray that had been cooked in the baker's oven and had a simple topping of mushrooms and anchovies.

As pizza became more popular, stalls were set up where the dough was shaped as customers ordered. Various toppings were invented. The tomato, which had arrived from the New World, was one of the most popular. The stalls soon developed into the pizzeria, an open air place for people to congregate, eat, drink and talk. This has gradually become the pizza parlors we have today, although the flavor of a pizza made, baked and cooked in the open air is unbeatable.

The dough for the pizza has been baked in other countries of the Mediterranean for just as long. The French have their own pissaladière recipe; for the Middle Eastern countries it's pita bread and Spain uses the dough as a pastry for spicy savory fillings. Even as far as China the same dough is steamed and served as individual stuffed snacks.

Although enjoying steady and constant popularity, it seems the pizza is now becoming a sophisticated, fashionable food with exotic toppings and unusual shapes. Who knows what will happen to the pizza in years to come!

INGREDIENTS

The traditional pizzas of Italy rely on the wonderful Mediterranean ingredients that are so plentiful—sun-ripened tomatoes, golden olive oil, fresh herbs and cheeses are the most well-known, but all sorts of other ingredients can be used as well.

Olive oil is indispensable for making genuine Italian flavored pizza.

Olives that are both green and ripe are used. Olive pulp is made from crushed ripe olives and is available in jars from gourmet shops and delicatessens.

Capers are buds from a flowering plant. They have a delicious, though distinct flavor, so use with care.

Oregano (wild marjoram) is used on many pizzas. Use fresh whenever possible.

Thyme, highly aromatic, can be used fresh or dried.

Parsley, both flat and curly, is used. Use only fresh parsley.

Basil is the most aromatic of all the Italian herbs. Use fresh whenever possible.

Sweet marjoram is added to pizzas after cooking.

Sage has a strong pronounced flavor. Use with care.

Mint should only be used fresh.

Black peppercorns should be freshly ground as the aroma disappears very quickly from the ready-ground type.

Nutmeg should be used freshly ground for the best flavor.

Chiles may be used fresh or dried.

Dried tomatoes in oil have an unusual, distinct flavor and are available from gourmet shops and delicatessens.

Cheeses. Mozzarella, Parmesan, Pecorino, Gorgonzola and Ricotta cheese are all used in pizzas. (Parmesan and Pecorino are at their best when freshly grated.)

— EQUIPMENT —

Flat pizza pan: Metal is essential to conduct the heat and ensure that the bottom of the pizza is crisp.

Baking sheet: This can be used as an alternative to the flat pizza pan, however, a rim should be formed at the edge of the dough to keep the filling in place.

Rectangular pan or jellyroll pan: Use this for making the traditional Roman pizza or any pizza that you wish to serve cut in squares.

Deep pizza pan: Use for the thick crust pizza. A cake pan or pie pan may be used instead.

Pizza cutter: This makes the job of cutting a pizza far easier than using a knife.

— TRADITIONAL PIZZA DOUGH —

2-3/4 cups bread flour
1 teaspoon salt
1 teaspoon active dried yeast
1 teaspoon sugar
About 3/4 cup warm water (110F, 45C)
1 tablespoon olive oil

Sift flour and salt into a medium bowl.

In a small bowl, combine yeast, sugar and 1/4 cup water; leave until frothy. Add yeast liquid to flour with remaining water and oil. Mix to a soft dough; knead on a floured surface 10 minutes until smooth. Place in a greased bowl; cover with plastic wrap. Let rise in a warm place 45 minutes or until doubled in size.

Punch down dough and knead briefly. Oil a 12-inch pizza pan. Place dough in center of pan; press out to edges with your knucles. Pinch up edges to make a rim. Use as directed in recipe.

VARIATIONS

If preferred, bake in a 14" x 10" jellyroll pan, or as 4 individual pizzas.

Herb or Nut Pizza Dough: Knead 2 tablespoons chopped fresh herbs (or 1 tablespoon dried herbs) into the dough. If preferred, knead 1 ounce chopped walnuts into the dough.

Whole-Wheat Pizza Dough: Use 2-1/4 cups whole-wheat flour and 1/4 cup wheat germ. Add extra water as required to form a soft dough.

Cornmeal Pizza Dough: Use 2-1/4 cups bread flour and 1/3 cup cornmeal.

POTATO PIZZA DOUGH

1 (5-oz.) potato
2-3/4 cups bread flour
1 teaspoon salt
1 teaspoon active dried yeast
1 teaspoon sugar
3/4 cup warm water (110F, 45C)

Scrub the unpeeled potato.

Boil in the skin 30 to 40 minutes or until tender when pierced with a fork. Drain and cool enough to remove the skin.

Sift flour and salt into a medium bowl. In a small bowl, cream fresh yeast with a little of the water and put in a warm place until frothy. If using dried active yeast, whisk together with the sugar and little water and set aside. If using easy blend yeast, mix into flour and salt at this stage (do not add any liquid).

Press potato through a sieve into flour; stir in yeast and remaining water.

Mix to a soft dough; and knead on a lightly floured surface 10 minutes until smooth. Place in a greased bowl; cover with plastic wrap. Let rise in a warm place about 45 minutes until doubled in size.

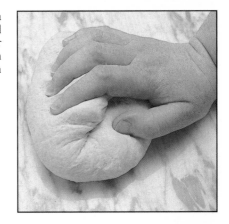

Punch down dough and knead briefly. Oil a 12-inch pizza pan. Place dough in the center of pan and press out to edges with your knuckles. Pinch up edges to make a rim. Use as directed in recipe.

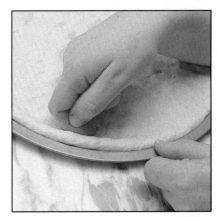

Variations: Knead 2 tablespoons chopped fresh herbs or 2 tablespoons freshly grated Parmesan cheese into the dough.

PAN PIZZA DOUGH

1-1/4 cups bread flour
1-1/4 cups all-purpose flour
1 teaspoon salt
1 teaspoon active dried yeast
1 teaspoon sugar
3/4 cup warm water (110F, 45C)

Make dough as for Traditional Pizza Dough, page 10. When dough has doubled in size, punch down and knead briefly.

Thoroughly oil a deep 10-inch pizza pan or cake pan. Place dough in the center of pan and press out to edges with your knuckles.

Cover with plastic wrap; let rise in a warm place about 1-1/2 hours or until almost to the top of pan. Use as directed in recipe.

CRUMBLE PIZZA DOUGH

1-1/2 cups all-purpose flour
1 teaspoon salt
2 teaspoons sugar
1/4 cup vegetable oil
6 teaspoons milk

Sift flour, salt and sugar into a medium bowl. Whisk oil and milk together in a measuring cup; pour onto flour mixture.

Stir with a fork until mixture is crumbly but still moist. It will not form a dough.

Press mixture onto bottom and up side of a deep 10-inch pizza pan or cake pan. Use as directed in recipe.

QUICK PIZZA DOUGH

1 cup whole-wheat flour
1 cup all purpose flour
2 teaspoons baking powder
Salt and pepper
1/4 cup butter or margarine
About 2/3 cup milk

Put flours and baking powder into a large bowl. Season to taste with salt and pepper. Add butter or margarine and rub in with fingertips until mixture resembles bread crumbs.

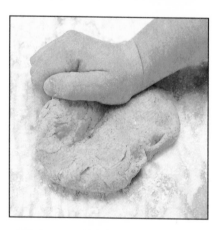

Stir in enough milk to form a dough. Turn onto a lightly floured surface; knead briefly.

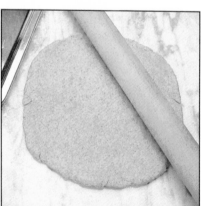

Roll out dough to a 10-inch circle. Transfer to a greased baking sheet. Use as directed in recipe.

Variation: Stir 2 tablespoons chopped fresh parsley into crumb mixture before adding milk.

Pizza Carcoifi

1 recipe Traditional Pizza Dough, shaped and ready for topping, pages 10 and 11

Topping:
2 tablespoons Tomato Topping, page 19
1/2 cup (2 oz.) shredded Fontina cheese
1 (6 oz.) jar marinated artichoke hearts
8 sun-dried tomatoes in oil
Salt and pepper
Parsley leaves, to garnish

Preheat oven to 425F (220C). Spread the dough with Tomato Topping. Sprinkle with cheese.

Drain artichokes, reserving oil. Drain tomatoes. Slice artichokes and arrange over the cheese. Chop tomatoes roughly and sprinkle over the artichokes. Season to taste with salt and pepper. Sprinkle with 1 to 2 tablespoons of the reserved oil.

Bake 20 minutes until dough is golden. Garnish with parsley. Makes 4 servings.

Pizza Napolitana

1 recipe Traditional Pizza Dough, shaped and ready for topping, pages 10 and 11

Topping:
3 tablespoons olive oil
1 pound tomatoes
1 garlic clove, crushed
Salt and pepper
8 ounces mozzarella cheese
1 (2-oz.) can anchovy fillets, drained
1 tablespoon chopped fresh oregano
Oregano leaves, to garnish

Preheat oven to 425F (220C). Brush dough with 1 tablespoon oil. Place tomatoes in a bowl. Pour enough boiling water over tomatoes to cover. Let stand 1 minute. Drain, peel and coarsely chop. Spread over dough. Sprinkle with garlic; season to taste with salt and pepper.

Slice cheese thinly. Arrange over tomatoes. Chop anchovies and sprinkle over cheese. Sprinkle with oregano and remaining oil. Bake 20 minutes until cheese has melted and dough is crisp and golden. Garnish with oregano leaves. Serve at once. Makes 4 servings.

Pizza Margherita

1 recipe Traditional Pizza Dough, pages
10 and 11

Tomato Topping:
1 pound tomatoes, peeled, page 18, or 1
(16-oz.) can tomatoes
2 tablespoons olive oil
1 onion, finely chopped
1 garlic clove, crushed
1 tablespoon tomato paste
1/2 teaspoon sugar
1 tablespoon chopped fresh basil
Salt and pepper

To Finish:
1 to 2 tablespoons olive oil
4 ounces mozzarella cheese
6 to 8 fresh basil leaves
Basil sprig, to garnish

Make Tomato Topping. Chop tomatoes, if using fresh. Heat oil in a medium saucepan. Add onion and garlic; cook until soft. Stir in tomatoes, tomato paste, sugar and basil. Season to taste with salt and pepper. Cover pan and simmer 30 minutes until thick.

Preheat oven to 425F (220C). Lightly grease a 12-inch pizza pan. Punch down dough and knead briefly. Place in prepared pan and press out to edges with your knuckles. Brush dough with 1 tablespoon oil. Spoon Tomato Topping over dough. Slice cheese thinly. Arrange over sauce. Sprinkle with salt and pepper to taste, 2 or 3 basil leaves and remaining oil. Bake 20 minutes until cheese has melted and dough is crisp and golden. Sprinkle with remaining basil leaves. Garnish with basil sprig. Serve at once. Makes 4 servings.

Pizza Marinara

1 recipe Traditional Pizza Dough, shaped
    and ready for topping, pages 10 and
    11

Topping:
3 tablespoons olive oil
8 ounces tomatoes, peeled, page 18
3 large garlic cloves
Salt and pepper
Few capers, if desired

Preheat oven to 425F (220C). Brush
dough with 1 tablespoon oil.

Quarter tomatoes and discard seeds.
Chop coarsely and drain in a sieve.
Spread over dough. Cut garlic into
thick slices and sprinkle over tomatoes.

Season with salt and pepper. Sprinkle
with remaining oil. Bake 20 minutes
until dough is crisp and golden. Sprinkle with capers. Makes 4 servings.

Roman Pizza

1 recipe Traditional Pizza Dough, made up to end of step 2, pages 10 and 11

Topping:
3 tablespoons olive oil
2 large onions, chopped
1 pound tomatoes, peeled, page 18, or 1 (16-oz.) can tomatoes, drained, chopped
1 (6-oz.) can pimentos, drained
1 (2-oz.) can anchovy fillets
12 pitted ripe olives
Pimentos and olives, to garnish

Preheat oven to 425F (220C). Lightly grease a 14" x 10" jellyroll pan. Punch down dough and knead briefly. Place in prepared pan; press out to edges with your knuckles. Pinch up edges to make a rim.

In a saucepan, heat 2 tablespoons oil. Add onions; cook until soft. Chop tomatoes, if fresh, add to pan and cook 2 minutes. Spoon over dough. Slice pimentos in strips and arrange over tomatoes. Drain anchovies, cut in half lengthwise and arrange in a lattice pattern on top. Halve olives and place in gaps. Sprinkle with remaining oil.

Bake 20 minutes until dough is crisp and golden. Garnish with pimento and olives. Makes 4 servings.

Four Seasons Pizza

1 recipe Traditional Pizza Dough, made
up to end of step 2, pages 10 and 11

Topping:
3 tablespoons olive oil
2 ounces button mushrooms
2 ounces prosciutto (Parma ham)
6 pitted ripe olives
4 canned artichoke hearts, drained
2 ounces mozzarella cheese
1 tomato, peeled, page 18
Salt and pepper

Preheat oven to 425F (220C). Lightly grease a baking sheet. Punch down dough and knead briefly. Place dough on baking sheet. Press out with your knuckles to a 10-inch circle. Brush dough with a little oil.

Heat 2 tablespoons oil in a medium saucepan. Add mushrooms; cook 5 minutes. Mark dough into 4 equal sections with a knife. Arrange mushrooms over one section. Cut ham in strips and chop olives; sprinkle over second section. Slice artichokes thinly. Arrange over third section. Slice cheese and tomato and arrange over fourth section. Season to taste with salt and pepper. Drizzle with remaining oil. Bake 20 minutes until dough is crisp and golden. Serve at once. Makes 4 servings.

Variation: Make this recipe as 4 individual pizzas, if preferred.

Spicy Pork & Pepper Pizza

1 recipe Traditional Pizza Dough, shaped and ready for topping, pages 10 and 11

Topping:
2 tablespoons olive oil
1 recipe Tomato Topping, see page 19
1 cup (4 oz.) mozzarella cheese
3 to 4 Italian pork sausages
Salt and pepper
1 yellow bell pepper, chopped
2 tablespoons freshly grated Parmesan cheese
Chopped fresh parsley, to garnish

Preheat oven to 425F (220C). Brush dough with 1 tablespoon oil. Spread Tomato Topping over dough. Sprinkle cheese on top. With a sharp knife, cut skins from sausages and discard. Cut meat into pieces; scatter over cheese. Season to taste with salt and pepper.

Sprinkle with chopped bell pepper, Parmesan cheese and remaining oil. Bake 20 minutes until dough is crisp. Garnish with parsley. Makes 4 servings.

Prosciutto & Olive Pizza

1 recipe Traditional Pizza Dough, shaped
and ready for topping, pages 10 and
11

Topping:
6 ounces mozzarella cheese
4 slices prosciutto
2 tablespoons olive pulp, see note
2 tablespoons olive oil
Salt and pepper

To Garnish:
Prosciutto
Few olives
Basil sprigs

Preheat oven to 425F (220C). Make the
topping. Cut cheese and prosciutto into
cubes. Place in bowl with olive pulp.
Mix together and moisten with a little
oil if dry. Spread over dough. Season to
taste with salt and pepper and sprinkle
with remaining oil. Bake 20 minutes
until dough is crisp and golden. Garnish with curls of prosciutto, olives and
basil sprigs. Makes 4 servings.

Note: Olive pulp may be bought in jars
from gourmet shops.

Italian Sausage Pizza

**1 recipe Traditional Pizza Dough, shaped
and ready for topping, pages 10 and
11**

Topping:
2 tablespoons olive oil
1 recipe Tomato Topping, page 19
2 ounces mushrooms, finely sliced
3 spicy Italian sausages
**2 tablespoons freshly grated Pecorino
cheese**
Salt and pepper
**Grated Pecorino cheese and flat-leaf
parsley, to garnish**

Preheat oven to 425F (220C). Brush dough with 1 tablespoon oil. Spread Tomato Topping over dough and sprinkle with mushrooms. With a sharp knife, cut skins from the sausages and discard. Cut meat into pieces and arrange over mushrooms. Sprinkle with 2 tablespoons grated cheese. Season to taste with salt and pepper.

Sprinkle remaining oil over top. Bake 20 minutes until dough is crisp and golden. Serve garnished with additional grated Pecorino cheese and flat-leaf parsley. Makes 4 servings.

Three Pepper Pizza

1 recipe Traditional Pizza Dough, shaped
and ready for topping, pages 10 and
11

Topping:
1 red pepper
1 yellow bell pepper
1 green bell pepper
2 tomatoes, peeled, page 18
3 tablespoons olive oil
1 onion, finely chopped
1 garlic clove, crushed
Salt and pepper
Pinch of dried leaf oregano
Oregano sprigs and olives, to garnish

Make the topping. Peel peppers: spear one at a time with a fork and hold over a gas flame for 5 to 10 minutes until black and blistered. Or, halve and seed peppers. Place under preheated grill until black. Peel skin off with a knife.

Chop red pepper; quarter, seed and chop tomatoes. Put in a saucepan with 2 tablespoons oil, onion and garlic. Cook until soft. Preheat oven to 425F (220C). Brush dough with a little oil.

Spread red pepper mixture over dough. Season to taste with salt and pepper. Sprinkle with oregano. Cut remaining peppers in strips. Arrange over pizza. Season to taste with salt and pepper. Drizzle with remaining oil. Bake 20 minutes until dough is crisp and golden. Garnish with oregano sprigs and olives. Makes 4 servings.

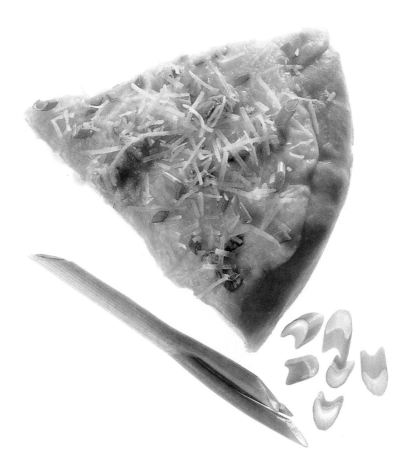

Four Cheese Pizza

1 recipe Traditional Pizza Dough, shaped and ready for topping, pages 10 and 11

Topping:
2 tablespoons olive oil
2 ounces mozzarella cheese
2 ounces Gorgonzola cheese
2 ounces Fontina or Gruyère cheese
1/2 cup freshly grated Parmesan cheese
Salt and pepper
Chopped green onion and grated Parmesan cheese, to garnish

Preheat oven to 425F (220C). Brush dough with 1 tablespoon oil. Cut the first 3 cheeses into small cubes. Scatter over the dough. Sprinkle with Parmesan cheese; season to taste with salt and pepper. Drizzle with remaining oil.

Bake 20 minutes until cheese is melted and dough is crisp and golden. Garnish with green onion and additional Parmesan cheese. Makes 4 servings.

English Muffin Pizzas

4 English muffins, halved
1/4 cup butter
2 tablespoons anchovy paste
4 tomatoes, sliced
8 slices processed Cheddar cheese
4 green onions
Stuffed olives
8 slices bacon, cooked until almost crisp

Preheat broiler. Toast muffins.

In a bowl, beat butter and anchovy paste together. Spread a little on each muffin half. Arrange tomato slices on halves.

Cut cheese slices diagonally into 4 triangular shapes. Arrange on top of muffin halves. Broil until cheese melts. Slice green onions and sprinkle on top. Spear olives with wooden picks. Roll up bacon; secure each roll with a pick with an olive. Use to garnish pizzas. Makes 4 servings.

Spicy Mushroom Muffins

4 whole-wheat English muffins

Topping:
2 tablespoons vegetable oil
1 tablespoon grated gingerroot, if desired
12 ounces mushrooms, sliced
1 bunch green onions, sliced
2 teaspoons Worcestershire sauce
1/2 teaspoon Dijon-style mustard
Salt and pepper
Butter for spreading, if desired
Green onion brushes, to garnish

Preheat oven to 425F (220C). Split muffins. Toast on both sides.

Meanwhile make topping. Heat oil in a large saucepan. Add gingerroot, if desired and cook for 10 to 15 seconds, stirring.

Add mushrooms; cook, stirring, for 1 minute. Add green onions and continue to cook 10 seconds. Add Worcestershire sauce and mustard. Season to taste with salt and pepper. Butter muffins, if desired. Spoon mushroom mixture on top of muffins. Bake 2 to 3 minutes. Garnish with onion brushes. Serve hot. Makes 4 servings.

Eggplant & Tomato Pizza

1 recipe Traditional Pizza Dough, shaped
    and ready for topping, pages 10 and
    11

Eggplant Topping:
1 pound eggplants
1 garlic clove, crushed
3 tablespoons lemon juice
3 tablespoons chopped fresh parsley
2 green onions, chopped
Salt and pepper

To Finish:
1 pound tomatoes, sliced
1 tablespoon olive oil
2 tablespoons chopped fresh parsley
2 tablespoons freshly grated Parmesan
    cheese
Parsley sprigs, to garnish

First make Eggplant Topping. Preheat
oven to 350F (175C). Put eggplants on
a baking sheet and bake 30 minutes
until soft. Cool. Halve and scoop out
soft centers into a bowl. Add garlic,
lemon juice, parsley and green onions.
Season to taste with salt and pepper.

Increase oven temperature to 425F
(220C). Spread Eggplant Topping over
dough. Arrange sliced tomatoes on top,
brush with oil and season to taste with
salt and pepper. Sprinkle with chopped
parsley and Parmesan cheese. Bake 20
minutes until crust is golden. Garnish
with parsley sprigs. Makes 4 servings.

Note: Eggplant Topping may be made
in advance and refrigerated for 3 to 4
days. It is also delicious served as a dip
with hot toast or pita bread.

Nutty Vegetable Pizza

**1 recipe Quick Pizza Dough, shaped and
ready for topping, page 16
1/3 cup (2 oz.) chopped roasted peanuts**

Topping:
**1/4 small white cabbage
2 carrots
2 celery stalks
2 tablespoons French dressing
Salt and pepper
4 ounces feta cheese, cubed
Peanut and celery leaves, to garnish**

Preheat oven to 425F (220C). Sprinkle dough with the chopped peanuts and press in lightly. Bake 15 minutes.

Meanwhile, shred cabbage, grate carrots and slice celery thinly. Place vegetables in a bowl. Add the French dressing and season to taste with salt and pepper.

Spoon vegetables over the pizza. Arrange cubes of cheese on top. Return to oven and bake 10 minutes. Garnish with peanuts and celery leaves. Serve at once. Makes 4 servings.

Pesto & Mushroom Pizza

1 recipe Pan Pizza Dough, shaped and ready for topping, page 14

Pesto Topping:
1 large bunch fresh basil leaves
3 garlic cloves, peeled
1/3 cup (2 oz.) pine nuts
3 tablespoons freshly grated Parmesan cheese
Salt and pepper
2/3 cup olive oil
Boiling water

To Finish:
6 ounces button mushrooms, sliced
Olive oil
2/3 cup (3 oz.) mozzarella cheese
2/3 cup (2 oz.) freshly grated Parmesan cheese
Basil sprigs and pine nuts, to garnish

Preheat oven to 425F (220C). Make Topping. In a blender or food processor, process basil leaves, garlic, pine nuts and 3 tablespoons Parmesan cheese until chopped. Season to taste with salt and pepper. With motor running, add oil in a gentle stream; process until absorbed. Blend until smooth, adding a little boiling water if necessary, for a spreading consistency.

Spread topping over dough. Arrange mushrooms on top; brush with olive oil. Sprinkle with mozzarella cheese and Parmesan cheese. Bake 20 minutes until crust is golden. Garnish with basil sprigs and pine nuts. Makes 4 servings.

Note: Pesto can be made in advance and stored in a tightly covered jar in the refrigerator up to 6 days. Ready-made pesto may be bought in delicatessens and specialty food shops.

Tapenade & Pepper Pizza

1 recipe Pan Pizza Dough, shaped and
ready for topping, page 14

Tapenade Topping:
5 ounces pitted green olives
1 (2-oz.) can anchovy fillets
1 (2-oz.) canned tuna in oil, drained
1 oz. capers
1 garlic clove
1 teaspoon Dijon-style mustard
Olive oil
Salt and pepper
Lemon juice

To Finish:
1 green bell pepper, peeled, page 26
1 yellow bell pepper, peeled, page 26
Mint sprigs and a few capers, to garnish

Preheat oven to 425F (220C). Make the
topping. In a blender or food processor, process the olives, anchovy fillets
and oil, tuna, capers, garlic and mustard. Process to a rough-textured
puree. Add a little extra oil if necessary.
Season with salt and pepper and lemon
juice.

Cut bell peppers into strips and then
into diamond shapes. Spread tapenade
over dough. Arrange bell peppers
attractively on top. Drizzle a little more
oil over and season with pepper. Bake
20 minutes until crust is golden. Garnish with mint sprigs and capers. Makes
4 servings.

French Bread Pizza

1 medium French bread loaf
2 tablespoons olive oil
1 (16-oz.) can tomatoes
Salt and pepper
1 (6-oz.) can tuna in oil, drained
8 pimento-stuffed olives
1 cup (4 oz.) shredded Edam cheese
3 green onions, chopped

To Serve:
Green salad

Preheat oven to 350F (175C). Cut a slice from the top of French loaf along the whole length. Scoop out most of the soft crumb from bottom portion (this and the lid will not be required but can be used for bread crumbs).

Brush inside of loaf with half the oil. Drain tomatoes and reserve juice. Brush inside of loaf with juice. Place loaf on a baking sheet and bake 10 minutes.

Chop drained tomatoes and arrange half inside the loaf. Season to taste with salt and pepper. Flake tuna and spoon over tomatoes. Top with remaining tomatoes and season again with salt and pepper.

Halve olives and arrange on top. Sprinkle with cheese. Return to oven and bake 15 minutes. Sprinkle with chopped green onions and serve at once with salad. Makes 2 servings.

Cheese & Onion Pizzas

8 small pita breads

Cheese Topping:
2 tablespoons butter or margarine
2 tablespoons all-purpose flour
2 cups (8 oz.) shredded Cheddar cheese
1/3 cup milk
1 egg yolk
Pinch of dry mustard
Pinch of red (cayenne) pepper

To Finish:
3 green onions, chopped
2 eggs, hard-cooked, chopped
Hard-boiled egg slices and chives, to garnish

Preheat oven to 425F (220C). Make the topping. In a small saucepan, melt butter or margarine. Add flour and cook, stirring, until smooth. Stir in half the cheese, then half the milk. Repeat with remaining cheese and milk. Beat in egg yolk. Stir in mustard and pepper and mix well.

Grease a baking sheet. Place pita breads on greased baking sheet. Spread topping over them. Bake 10 minutes. In a small bowl, mix chopped green onions and chopped hard-cooked eggs together. Sprinkle the mixture over the pizzas and bake 2 minutes. Garnish each pizza with a hard-cooked egg slice and chives. Serve hot. Makes 4 servings.

Creamy Salmon Pizza

1 recipe Whole-Wheat Pizza Dough,
   shaped and ready for topping,
   pages 10 and 11

Topping:
1 (16-oz.) can red salmon
1 zucchini, finely chopped
3 tablespoons whipping cream
Salt and pepper
1 teaspoon grated lemon peel
1 tablespoon chopped fresh dill
Olive oil
1/4 cup (3/4 oz.) grated Parmesan cheese
Lemon peel and dill sprigs, to garnish

Preheat oven to 425F (220C). Make the topping. Drain salmon and discard bones. Put in a medium bowl and flake with a fork. Stir in zucchini, cream, salt and pepper to taste, lemon peel and dill.

Brush dough with olive oil. Spoon the salmon mixture on top. Sprinkle with the Parmesan cheese. Bake 20 minutes until crust is golden. Garnish with lemon peel and dill sprigs. Serve at once. Makes 4 servings.

Cheesy Seafood Pizza

1 recipe Traditional Pizza Dough, shaped
and ready for topping, pages 10 and
11

Topping:
1 recipe Cheese Topping, page 35
1 (6-oz.) can tuna, packed in water
6 ounces peeled small shrimp, thawed if
frozen
1/4 teaspoon paprika
Salt and pepper
Lemon twists, coriander sprigs and
peeled shrimp, to garnish

Preheat oven to 425F (220C). Spread
the Cheese Topping over the pizza
dough.

Drain tuna, put in a bowl and flake
roughly with a fork. Mix in shrimp and
paprika and season to taste with salt
and pepper. Spread mixture over the
Cheese Topping.

Bake 20 minutes until crust is crisp and
golden. Garnish with lemon twists,
coriander sprigs and peeled shrimp.
Makes 4 servings.

Frittata Pizza

1 recipe Traditional Pizza Dough, made
  up to end of Step 2, pages 10 and 11

Topping:
2 tablespoons olive oil
1 onion, thinly sliced
3 new potatoes, cooked, sliced
8 slices pepper salami
1 small green bell pepper, sliced
8 pitted ripe olives, halved
2 ounces feta cheese, cubed
1 tablespoon chopped fresh parsley
4 cherry tomatoes, halved
6 eggs
Salt and pepper
Watercress to garnish

Preheat oven to 425F (220C). Grease a
deep 10-inch pizza pan or cake pan.
Punch down risen dough and knead
briefly, then press dough into pan.

Brush dough with a little of the oil.
Arrange sliced onion over the top.
Sprinkle with remaining oil. Bake 10
minutes.

Remove pizza from oven. Arrange
sliced potatoes, salami, bell pepper,
olives and cheese over the surface. Add
parsley and tomatoes. In a bowl, beat
together eggs and season to taste with
salt and pepper. Pour over pizza and
bake for 10 to 15 minutes until topping
is puffed and golden. Garnish with
watercress. Makes 4 servings.

Tomato & Mint Pizza

1 recipe Quick Pizza Dough, shaped and ready for topping, page 16

Topping:
1 tablespoon vegetable oil
8 ounces cherry tomatoes
Salt and pepper
1 large onion, sliced thinly
3/4 cup (3 oz.) shredded Cheddar cheese
2 tablespoons chopped fresh mint
Mint sprigs, to garnish
Plain yogurt, to serve

Preheat oven to 425F (220C). Brush dough with oil. Halve tomatoes and arrange over dough. Season to taste with salt and pepper. Arrange onion slices on top. Sprinkle with shredded cheese and chopped mint.

Bake 20 minutes until crust is golden brown and cheese is bubbling. Garnish with mint sprigs. Serve at once, with yogurt. Makes 4 servings.

Gravlax Muffins

6 English muffins

Topping:
1/2 cup butter, softened
1 teaspoon honey
1 teaspoon Dijon-style mustard
2 teaspoons lemon juice
1 tablespoon chopped fresh dill
Salt and pepper
12 ounces gravlax or smoked salmon
Dairy sour cream and dill sprigs

Preheat oven to 425F (220C). Halve the muffins and place them on a baking sheet. Bake 5 minutes.

Meanwhile, in a bowl beat the butter with the honey, mustard, lemon juice, and chopped dill. Season to taste with salt and pepper.

Spread the butter mixture over the muffins and top with the gravlax or smoked salmon, dividing it equally between them. Bake 5 minutes, then serve at once with sour cream and dill sprigs. Makes 6 servings.

Avocado & Crab Bites

1 recipe Traditional Pizza Dough, made up to end of step 2, pages 10 and 11

Topping:
2 avocados
1 tablespoon lemon juice
1/4 cup butter
1/2 cup all-purpose flour
1-1/4 cups milk
Salt and pepper
1/4 teaspoon red (cayenne) pepper
12 ounces crabmeat, thawed if frozen, drained
1/2 cup (2 oz.) shredded Gruyère cheese
Avocado slices and tomato, to garnish

Preheat oven to 425F (220C). Punch down dough and knead briefly. Roll out dough and use to line a 14" x 10" jellyroll pan.

Make topping. Halve avocados; remove stones. Scoop out flesh and chop coarsely. Place in a bowl with lemon juice and stir lightly to coat. Set aside.

Melt butter in a saucepan. Stir in flour and cook for 2 minutes. Stir in milk; bring to a boil. Reduce heat; simmer 2 minutes. Season to taste with salt and pepper and cayenne.

Remove pan from heat. Stir in crab, cheese, and chopped avocado. Spread over the dough, then bake 20 minutes until crust is golden. Cool slightly before cutting into fingers or squares. Garnish with avocado slices and tomato. Makes 6 to 8 servings.

Coronation Chicken Pizza

1 recipe Traditional Pizza Dough, shaped
and ready for topping, pages 10 and
11

Topping:
12 ounces cooked chicken, cubed
1/3 cup (2 oz.) roasted cashew nuts
1 small leek, finely shredded
3 tablespoons mayonnaise
3 tablespoons plain yogurt
1 teaspoon curry powder
1 tablespoon apricot jam
1 tablespoon mango chutney, chopped
2 tablespoons chopped cilantro
Salt and pepper
Lemon juice
Cilantro, to garnish

Preheat oven to 425F (220C). Make the
topping. In a bowl, mix chicken, cashew
nuts and leek. In a second bowl, mix
mayonnaise, yogurt, curry powder,
jam, chutney and cilantro. Season to
taste with salt and pepper and lemon
juice. Mix sauce with the chicken mixture. Spoon mixture on top of the
dough. Bake 20 minutes until the crust
is golden. Garnish with cilantro. Serve
at once. Makes 4 servings.

Variation: Substitute other cooked and
cubed meat, such as ham, pork, or lamb
for the chicken and use roasted
almonds for the cashew nuts.

Tarragon Trout Package

1 recipe Potato Pizza Dough, made up to
   end of step 5, pages 12 and 13

Filling:
1 pound trout fillets, skinned
2-1/2 cups white wine
Few parsley and tarragon sprigs
Salt and pepper
1/4 cup butter
1/2 cup all-purpose flour
2 tablespoons half and half
4 ounces peeled shrimp, thawed if frozen
2 ounces mushrooms, sliced
Beaten egg, to glaze
4 teaspoons sesame seeds
Shrimp, lemon wedges and tarragon
   sprigs, to garnish

Make the filling. Put the fish and wine in a saucepan with parsley and tarragon sprigs and season with a little salt and pepper. Bring to a boil, cover and remove from the heat. Let cool. Drain and reserve liquid. Flake fish.

Melt butter in a saucepan. Add flour and cook, stirring, until bubbly. Add reserved liquid to make a smooth sauce. Remove from heat, stir in fish, half and half, shrimp and mushrooms. Taste for seasoning. Cool.

Preheat oven to 425F (220C). Grease a baking sheet. Punch down dough and knead briefly. Roll out dough on a lightly floured surface to a 12-inch square. Place on baking sheet. Spoon filling in center. Brush edges with beaten egg. Fold corners of dough to center; pinch seams to seal. Brush with beaten egg and sprinkle with sesame seeds. Bake 25 to 30 minutes. Garnish with shrimp, lemon and tarragon. Makes 4 to 6 servings.

Ham & Tomato Bites

**1 recipe Traditional Pizza Dough, made
to end of step 2, pages 10 and 11**

Topping:
**1 recipe Tomato Topping, page 19
12 to 14 slices prosciutto
6 ounces mozzarella cheese, sliced
Olives, anchovies and thyme sprigs, to
    garnish**

Preheat oven to 425F (220C). Grease
several baking sheets. Roll out dough
very thinly and cut out 12 to 14 circles
with a 1-1/2- to 2-inch cutter.

Spread dough with Tomato Topping.
Top each circle with a ham slice and a
mozzarella cheese slice. Bake 10 to 12
minutes until the crust is golden and
the cheese has melted. Garnish with
olives, anchovies and thyme. Serve at
once. Makes 6 to 8 servings.

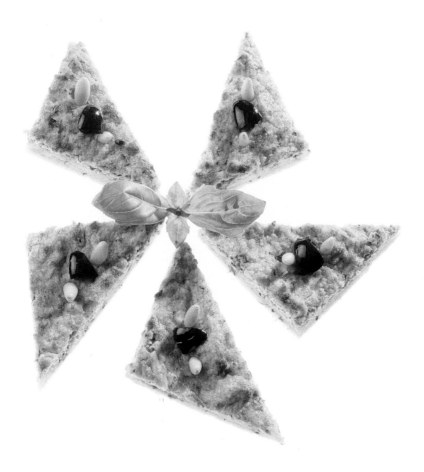

Pesto Pizzelle

**1 recipe Traditional Pizza Dough, made
to end of step 2, pages 10 and 11**

Topping:
6 ounces ricotta cheese
3 tablespoons Pesto Topping, page 32
1 egg, beaten
**Basil sprigs, ripe olives and pine nuts, to
garnish**

Preheat oven to 425F (220C). Punch down dough and knead briefly. Roll out dough and use to line a 14" x 10" jellyroll pan.

Make the topping. Beat together ricotta cheese and Pesto Topping and egg to make a smooth, firm mixture.

Spread over the dough, then bake 20 minutes until crust is golden. Cool slightly, then cut into squares or triangles. Garnish with basil, olives and pine nuts. Serve as a cocktail snack. Makes 10 to 15 servings.

Fresh Herb Pizza

**1 recipe Quick Pizza Dough, shaped and
ready for topping, page 16**

Topping:
**2 tablespoons olive oil
1 tablespoon chopped fresh basil
1 tablespoon chopped fresh parsley
1 teaspoon chopped fresh oregano
1-1/2 cups (6 oz.) shredded mozzarella
cheese
3/4 cup (2-1/4 oz.) grated Pecorino cheese
Salt and pepper
Fresh herbs, to garnish**

Preheat oven to 425F (220C). Brush the
dough with 1 tablespoon oil. Sprinkle
with chopped herbs. Cover with the
cheese and season to taste with salt and
pepper. Drizzle with remaining oil.
Bake 20 minutes until golden. Garnish
with herbs. Makes 4 servings.

Asparagus Ham Squares

**1 recipe Traditional Pizza Dough, made
up to end of step 2, pages 10 and 11**
1 tablespoon vegetable oil

Topping:
6 ounces sliced ham
6 ounces ricotta cheese
2 tablespoons milk
**1 (10-oz.) package frozen asparagus
spears, thawed**
Salt and pepper
Freshly grated Parmesan cheese

Preheat oven to 425F (220C). Grease a 14" x 10" jellyroll pan. Punch down dough and knead briefly. Roll out dough on a lightly floured surface and use to line bottom and sides of pan. Prick bottom with a fork. Brush with oil. Bake 15 minutes until crisp and golden.

Meanwhile, finely chop 4 ounces ham. In a medium bowl, combine chopped ham, cheese and milk. Cut tips from asparagus and reserve. Chop stalks and stir into cheese mixture.

Remove pizza from oven and cool slightly. Spread cheese mixture over dough. Slice remaining ham in strips and arrange in a lattice pattern over dough. Dot asparagus tips on surface, season to taste with salt and pepper and sprinkle with Parmesan cheese. Return to oven and cook 2 minutes. Slide pizza from pan onto a chopping board. With a sharp knife cut off crusts and discard. Cut pizza into small squares or fingers and serve as a cocktail snack. Makes 8 to 10 servings.

Ratatouille & Shrimp Pizza

**1 recipe Whole-Wheat Pizza Dough,
shaped and ready for topping, pages
10 and 11
1 tablespoon vegetable oil**

Topping:
**2 tablespoons vegetable oil
1 large onion, chopped
2 garlic cloves, crushed
3 small zucchini, halved
1 small red bell pepper
1 small green bell pepper
1 small yellow bell pepper
8 ounces eggplant, cubed
1 (16-oz.) can tomatoes
2 tablespoons tomato paste
Salt and pepper
4 ounces peeled shrimp, thawed if frozen
Chopped parsley, to garnish**

Make the topping. Heat oil in a large
saucepan. Add onion and garlic. Cook
3 minutes, stirring. Do not burn garlic.

Cut zucchini and bell peppers into 1/2-
inch pieces. Add to pan with eggplant.
Drain juice from tomatoes; reserve.
Add chopped tomatoes and juice,
tomato paste and season to taste with
salt and pepper. Stir well and cook 15
minutes until vegetables are cooked
and the sauce thickened.

Preheat oven to 425F (220C). Prick
dough with a fork and brush with oil.
Bake 15 minutes. Stir shrimp into
vegetables and spoon on top of crust.
Bake 5 minutes. Serve at once sprinkled
with parsley. Makes 4 servings.

Mixed Seafood Pizza

1 recipe Traditional Pizza Dough, shaped
   and ready for topping, pages 10 and
   11

Topping:
8 ounces mussels in the shell
2 tablespoons olive oil
2 garlic cloves, crushed
4 ounces squid, cleaned
1 (16-oz.) can chopped tomatoes
Salt and pepper
4 ounces shrimp, cooked, peeled, thawed
   if frozen
8 ounces clean shelled clams or 1 (14-oz.)
   can clams, drained
2 tablespoons chopped fresh parsley
Flat-leaf parsley and lemon, to garnish

Make topping. Scrub mussels and re-move beards. Place in a large saucepan with 2 tablespoons water. Cover and cook over medium heat, shaking pan, until all the shells are open.

Strain pan juice and reserve. In a sauce-pan, heat 1 tablespoon oil and garlic. Slice squid and add to pan. Cook 5 min-utes, stirring. Remove squid with a slot-ted spoon and reserve. Discard garlic. Add tomatoes, reserved mussel juice and season to taste with salt and pep-per. Cook gently 30 minutes.

Preheat oven to 425F (220C). Brush dough with remaining oil; prick with a fork. Bake 15 to 20 minutes until gold-en. Add shrimp and clams to sauce. Cook 10 minutes. Stir in squid and mussels. Remove pizza from oven. Spoon sauce over crust, sprinkle with parsley and return to oven for 10 min-utes. Garnish with parsley and lemon, serve at once. Makes 4 servings.

Pizza Canapés

1 recipe Cornmeal Pizza Dough, made up to end of step 2, pages 10 and 11
1 tablespoon olive oil

Topping:
1 recipe Cheese Topping, page 35
Selection of the following: anchovy fillets, stuffed and plain; olives; capers; lumpfish roe; cooked shrimp; smoked salmon; crisp bacon; smoked quail eggs; sprigs of fresh herbs

Preheat oven to 425F (220C). Grease several baking sheets. Punch down dough and knead briefly. Roll out dough very thinly and cut out 10 to 12 small circles with a 1-1/2- to 2-inch cutter. Spread with a little Cheese Topping and arrange on baking sheets. Bake in the oven 10 to 15 minutes until golden. Top with desired toppings and serve at once. Makes 10 to 12 servings.

Ham & Cheese Party Pizzas

**1 recipe Cornmeal Pizza Dough; made
up to end of step 2; pages 10 and 11**
1 tablespoon olive oil

Topping:
1 recipe Tomato Topping, page 19
12 slices prosciutto
10 to 12 pitted ripe or green olives
Freshly grated Parmesan cheese
Thyme sprigs, to garnish

Preheat oven to 425F (220C). Grease several baking sheets. Punch down dough and knead briefly. Roll out dough and cut as for Pizza Canapés, see page 50. Brush with oil and bake 15 to 20 minutes until golden.

Spread each circle with a little Tomato Topping. Cut prosciutto into 10 to 12 pieces. Fold each piece into a cone shape and place on top of a circle. Place an olive in each cone and sprinkle with Parmesan cheese. Return to oven for 3 minutes to soften cheese. Garnish with thyme. Serve at once. Makes 10 to 12 servings.

Gorgonzola & Nut Shapes

1 recipe Traditional Pizza Dough, made up to end of step 2, pages 10 and 11

Topping:
6 ounces Gorgonzola cheese
6 ounces mozzarella cheese
10 walnut halves
3 tablespoons walnut oil
Cucumber, to garnish

Preheat oven to 425F (220C). Grease a 14" x 10" jellyroll pan. Punch down dough and knead briefly. Roll out dough on a lightly floured surface and use to line bottom and sides of pan.

Cut cheeses into small cubes. Coarsely chop walnuts. Brush surface of dough with a little walnut oil. Sprinkle cheese over dough and top with walnuts. Drizzle with remaining oil.

Bake 20 minutes until dough is crisp and golden. Slide from pan onto a cutting board. Cut crusts off with a sharp knife and discard. Cut pizza into small squares and fingers. Garnish with cucumber and serve at once as a cocktail snack. Makes 8 to 10 servings.

Mozzolive Bites

1 recipe Cornmeal Pizza Dough, made up
   to end of step 2, pages 10 and 11

Topping:
4 tablespoons olive oil
6 ounces mozzarella cheese
1 (5-1/2-oz.) jar olive paste
Salt and pepper
Sage leaves and pimento, to garnish

Preheat oven to 425F (220C). Grease
several baking sheets. Punch down
dough and knead briefly. Roll out
dough and cut as for Pizza Canapés, see
page 50. Brush with 1 tablespoon oil
and bake 15 to 20 minutes until golden.

Cut cheese into tiny pieces and place in
a medium bowl. Stir in the olive paste.
Season to taste with salt and pepper.
Spoon a little of the mixture onto each
circle, dividing it equally among them.

Drizzle with remaining oil. Bake 3 to 4
minutes until cheese melts. Garnish
with sage leaves and pimento. Serve at
once as a cocktail snack. Makes 10 to 12
servings.

Artichoke & Cheese Pizza

1 recipe Traditional Pizza Dough, shaped and ready for topping, pages 10 and 11

Topping:
3 tablespoons olive oil
1 (14-oz.) can artichoke hearts
Salt and pepper
2 cups (8 oz.) shredded Emmental cheese
Marjoram leaves and sliced pimento, to garnish

Preheat oven to 425F (220C). Brush the pizza dough with 1 tablespoon of the oil.

Drain artichokes and slice thinly. Arrange artichoke slices over dough. Sprinkle with remaining oil; season to taste with salt and pepper. Sprinkle the cheese over the top.

Bake 20 minutes until crust is crisp and golden and cheese has melted. Garnish with marjoram leaves and sliced pimento. Serve at once. Makes 4 servings.

Three Salami Pizza

1 recipe Quick Pizza Dough, shaped and
    ready for topping, page 16

Topping:
1 tablespoon vegetable oil
3 tomatoes, finely chopped
Salt and pepper
6 ounces mixed sliced salami
1/2 cup (2 oz.) shredded Cheddar cheese
Gherkins, to garnish

Preheat oven to 425F (220C). Brush
dough with the oil.

Spread tomatoes over dough. Season to
taste with salt and pepper. Cut salami
into strips and arrange over tomatoes.
Sprinkle with cheese. Bake 20 minutes
until dough is golden and cheese
melted. Garnish with gherkins. Makes
4 servings.

Mushroom & Cheese Pizza

**1 recipe Whole-Wheat Pizza Dough,
shaped and ready for topping, pages
10 and 11**

Topping:
**1 to 2 tablespoons Dijon-style mustard or
2 tablespoons butter or margarine,
melted
4 ounces sliced ham
4 ounces mushrooms, sliced
6 tablespoons sieved tomatoes
1 cup (4 oz.) shredded Cheddar cheese
Salt and pepper
Watercress sprigs, to garnish**

Preheat oven to 425F (220C). Spread dough with the mustard, if using, or brush with the melted butter or margarine.

Slice the ham diagonally to form diamond shapes. Arrange over dough. Place one-third of the mushrooms in the center and the remainder in groups around the edge of the pizza. Spoon a little tomato over mushrooms. Sprinkle with cheese. Season to taste with salt and pepper. Bake 20 minutes until crust is crisp and golden and the cheese bubbling. Garnish with watercress. Makes 6 servings.

Sausage & Onion Pizza

1 recipe Traditional Pizza Dough, shaped
and ready for topping, pages 10 and
11

Topping:
1 pound Italian sausages
2 tablespoons butter or margarine
1 large onion, finely sliced
4 ounces mushrooms, quartered
4 tablespoons sieved tomatoes
Celery leaves, to garnish

Preheat oven to 425F (220C). Make
topping. Cook sausages in a large skillet
until no longer pink in center. Meanwhile, melt butter in a saucepan and
cook onion until soft. Add mushrooms
and tomatoes and cook, stirring, 5 minutes. Drain sausages on paper towels.
Slice diagonally.

Spoon the onion mixture over dough
and top with sausage slices. Bake 20
minutes until crust is crisp and golden.
Garnish with celery leaves. Makes 6
servings.

Sausage & Apple Pizza

1 recipe Whole-Wheat Pizza Dough, made up to end of step 2, pages 10 and 11
2 tablespoons vegetable oil

Topping:
1 pound pork sausages with herbs
1 Granny Smith apple
3 tablespoons apple juice or cider
2 tablespoons mild mustard
Salt and pepper
1 Red Delicious apple
1 Granny Smith apple
Lemon juice

To Serve:
1 small package potato chips

Preheat oven to 425F (220C). Lightly grease a 14" x 10" jellyroll pan. Punch down dough and knead briefly. Place in pan and press over bottom and up sides. Brush with 1 tablespoon oil.

Remove skin from the sausages by splitting with a sharp knife. Put sausage meat in a medium bowl. Grate 1 Granny Smith apple, stir into sausage with apple juice or cider and mustard and season to taste with salt and pepper. Spread the mixture evenly over dough.

Core remaining apples. Slice thinly and brush cut surfaces with lemon juice. Arrange over sausage mixture and brush with remaining oil. Bake 20 minutes until crust is crisp and golden. Crush potato chips coarsely and sprinkle over top of pizza. Makes 6 servings.

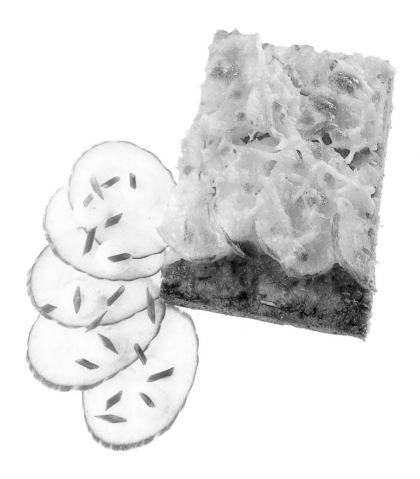

Potato Pizza Squares

1 recipe Whole-Wheat Pizza Dough,
  made up to end of step 2, pages 10
  and 11

Topping:
8 small potatoes, peeled
Salt
1 tablespoon vegetable oil
1 recipe Tomato Topping, see page 19
1/2 cup (2 oz.) shredded Cheddar cheese
Cucumber slices and sliced green onion,
  to garnish

Cook potatoes in salted boiling water in a medium saucepan 10 to 15 minutes. Drain, cool slightly, then slice thinly.

Meanwhile, preheat oven to 425F (220C). Grease a 14" x 10" jellyroll pan. Punch down dough and knead briefly. Roll out and use to line pan. Brush with oil.

Spread Tomato Topping over dough. Arrange potato slices on top and sprinkle with cheese. Bake 20 minutes. Serve cut into squares, garnish with cucumber and green onion. Makes 6 to 8 servings.

Pizza Faces

Freshly-baked or bought, ready-made individual pizza crusts

Topping:
1/4 cup tomato sauce or chutney
6 to 8 processed Cheddar cheese slices
Alfalfa sprouts or grated carrot
Olive slices
Wide bell pepper strips
Herb sprigs

Preheat oven to 425F (220C). Spread pizza crusts with tomato sauce or chutney. Arrange cheese over top to represent skin. Place on a baking sheet and bake 10 to 15 minutes until cheese is melted.

Give each child the baked pizza and ingredients to make his own pizza face, using alfalfa sprouts or carrot as hair, olive slices for eyes, bell pepper strips for mouth and herb sprigs for nose. Makes 2 servings.

Variations: Many other ingredients can be used in place of those listed and children can make different expressions on the faces.

BLT Pizza

1 recipe Traditional Pizza Dough, shaped and ready for topping, pages 10 and 11

Filling:
8 bacon slices, crisp-cooked
4 tomatoes, coarsely chopped
1/2 small iceberg lettuce head
4 to 6 tablespoons mayonnaise
Salt and pepper
Shredded lettuce, to garnish

Preheat oven to 425F (220C). With kitchen scissors, cut bacon into pieces. Very finely shred the lettuce. In a bowl, mix bacon, tomatoes, lettuce and mayonnaise and season to taste with salt and pepper.

Spread the mixture over the dough. Bake 20 minutes. Garnish with additional shredded lettuce. Serve at once. Makes 4 servings.

Ham & Pineapple Pizza

6 English muffins, halved

Topping:
1 recipe Cheese Topping, page 35
6 ounces ham, minced or finely chopped
Salt and pepper
1 (14-oz.) can pineapple slices in juice
Chopped parsley, pineapple chunks and
cherries to garnish

Preheat oven to 425F (220C). Toast muffin halves. Spread cheese topping on one side of each muffin half. Sprinkle with two-thirds of minced or chopped ham. Season to taste with salt and pepper. Drain pineapple. Arrange pineapple slices on top of ham. Fill pineapple centers with remaining ham. Bake 20 minutes until hot and cheese is melted. Sprinkle with chopped parsley. Garnish with pineapple chunks and cherries on wooden picks. Makes 6 servings.

Breakfast Pizza

1 recipe Traditional Pizza Dough, shaped and ready for topping, pages 10 and 11

Topping:
1 tablespoon vegetable oil
1 (16-oz.) can tomatoes, drained, chopped
Salt and pepper
8 bacon slices, partially cooked
4 eggs

Preheat oven to 425F (220C). Brush dough with 1 tablespoon oil.

Spoon chopped tomatoes over dough. Season to taste with salt and pepper. Arrange bacon over the tomatoes, leaving 4 holes, equally spaced for eggs. Bake 15 minutes.

Remove from oven. Break an egg into each of the 4 holes. Return pizza to oven about 10 minutes until the whites are set but the yolks still liquid. Serve at once. Makes 4 servings.

Ground Beef & Onion Pizza

1 recipe Potato Pizza Dough, shaped and
   ready for topping, pages 12 and 13

Topping:
8 ounces lean ground beef
Salt and pepper
2 tablespoons tomato paste
2 tablespoons Worcestershire sauce
2 tablespoons vegetable oil
4 ounces mushrooms, sliced
1 green bell pepper, sliced in rings
1 small onion, sliced crosswise
Watercress, chives and red bell pepper,
   to garnish

Make the topping. In a medium saucepan, cook the beef until browned; drain
off any fat. Season to taste with salt and
pepper. Add tomato paste and Worcestershire sauce. Cook 15 minutes, stirring the mixture occasionally.

Preheat oven to 425F (220C). Brush
dough with 1 tablespoon oil. Arrange
mushrooms on dough. Spoon meat
mixture on top. Arrange rings of bell
pepper and onion over meat mixture
and brush with remaining oil. Bake 20
minutes until crust is crisp and golden.
Garnish with watercress bunches tied
with chives and red bell pepper. Makes
4 servings.

Sardine & Tomato Pizza

1 recipe Traditional Pizza Dough, shaped and ready for topping, pages 10 and 11

Topping:
4 tablespoons tomato sauce
1 (4-oz.) can sardines in oil, drained
2 tomatoes, sliced
4 processed cheese slices
Cress sprouts, to garnish

Preheat oven to 425F (220C). Spread tomato sauce over the dough. Split sardines horizontally and arrange around the edge. Make a circle of overlapping tomatoes in the center.

Cut cheese strips and arrange in a lattice over the tomatoes. Bake 20 minutes until the crust is golden. Garnish with sprouts. Serve hot. Makes 6 servings.

Bolognese Pizza

1 recipe Potato Pizza Dough, with Parmesan cheese, shaped and ready for topping, pages 12 and 13

Topping:
2 tablespoons vegetable oil
3 bacon slices, chopped
1 onion, finely chopped
1 carrot, finely chopped
1 stalk celery, finely chopped
1 garlic clove, crushed
8 ounces lean ground beef
1 tablespoon tomato paste
1/4 teaspoon Italian seasoning
1/2 cup beef stock
Salt and pepper

To Serve:
Freshly grated Parmesan cheese
Tomato and marjoram sprigs, to garnish

Make the topping. In a medium saucepan, heat oil; add bacon. Cook 2 minutes. Add onion, carrot, celery and garlic. Cook, stirring, until soft. Add ground beef and cook, stirring until brown. Drain off fat.

Stir in tomato paste, Italian seasoning and stock; season to taste with salt and pepper. Cover and simmer 30 minutes.

Preheat oven to 425F (220C). Spoon sauce on top of dough. Bake 20 minutes until crust is crisp and golden. Sprinkle with Parmesan cheese and garnish with tomato and marjoram. Makes 6 servings.

Tuna & Onion Pizza

1 recipe Pan Pizza Dough, shaped and ready for topping, page 14

Topping:
2 tablespoons vegetable oil
1 (16-oz.) can chopped tomatoes
1 bunch green onions, chopped
1 (7-oz.) can tuna, drained
Salt and pepper

Preheat oven to 425F (220C). Brush dough with 1 tablespoon oil. Bake 20 minutes until golden.

Make the topping. Drain tomatoes, reserving juice. Chop tomatoes. In a medium saucepan, heat the chopped tomatoes and remaining oil. Add half the onions to pan; cook 10 minutes. Flake tuna; stir into tomato mixture. Season to taste with salt and pepper.

Spoon onto dough and bake in the oven 3 to 5 minutes. Shred remaining onions; sprinkle over pizza to serve. Makes 6 servings.

Steak & Kidney Pizza

**1 recipe Traditional Pizza Dough, shaped
and ready for topping, see pages 10
and 11**

Topping:
**1 pound sirloin steak, trimmed
8 ounces lambs' kidneys
2 tablespoons vegetable oil
1 onion, chopped
1 tablespoon all-purpose flour
2/3 cup beef stock
2/3 cup red wine
Salt and pepper
1/2 teaspoon dried leaf thyme
Thyme sprigs, to garnish**

Cut steak in even-sized strips. Halve kidneys, remove cores and cut each half into 2 pieces. Heat oil in a large saucepan and cook onion 5 minutes until golden. Remove with slotted spoon and reserve.

Brown meat in oil, a little at a time. Using a slotted spoon, remove meat as soon as it is cooked and reserve. Add flour to pan and stir well, scraping up browned bits. Stir in stock and wine. Season to taste with salt and pepper. Add thyme, bring to a boil, then reduce heat and cook until thickened.

Meanwhile, preheat oven to 425F (220C). Return meat and onion to pan, stir well, then spoon on top of pizza, reserving a little sauce. Bake 15 minutes, spoon over reserved sauce and bake 5 minutes. Garnish with thyme. Serve hot. Makes 4 to 6 servings.

Oriental Chicken Pizza

1 recipe Traditional Pizza Dough, made
up to end of step 2, pages 10 and 11

Topping:
2 skinned, boneless chicken breasts
1 onion, finely chopped
2 garlic cloves, crushed
2 tablespoons soy sauce
1 tablespoon lemon juice
2 teaspoons brown sugar
4 ounces bean sprouts

Sauce:
2/3 cup coconut milk
1-3/4 cups boiling water
1 teaspoon coriander seeds
1 teaspoon cumin seeds
2 garlic cloves, crushed
1/2 cup crunchy peanut butter
1 teaspoon brown sugar
1 fresh green chile, seeded, finely
chopped
3 tablespoons lemon juice
Green onion, parsley and cucumber, to
garnish

Make the topping. Cut chicken into
matchstick strips. Place in a medium
glass bowl. Add onion, garlic, soy sauce,
lemon juice, sugar and bean sprouts.
Mix well; let stand for 20 minutes.

Make the sauce. Mix coconut milk and
boiling water together in a small bowl.
Set aside. Crush spices; put in a
medium saucepan. Heat gently. Stir in
rest of sauce ingredients, cover and
simmer 10 minutes.

Meanwhile, preheat oven to 425F
(220C). Grease a baking sheet. Punch
down dough and knead briefly. Put
dough in center of baking sheet and
press out to edges. Pinch up edges to
make a rim. Spoon chicken mixture
over dough. Bake 15 to 20 minutes until golden. Garnish with onion, parsley
and cucumber. Serve with sauce. Makes
4 servings.

French Brie Pizza

1 recipe Traditional Pizza Dough, with walnuts, shaped and ready for topping, pages 10 and 11

Topping:
2 small leeks, finely shredded
2 tablespoons walnut or olive oil
Salt
8 ounces Brie or Camembert cheese, thinly sliced
1 teaspoon green peppercorns, drained
2 tablespoons chopped walnuts

Preheat oven to 425F (220C). Make the topping. Put leeks in a medium saucepan with 1 tablespoon oil. Cook gently 5 minutes, stirring, until soft. Brush dough with remaining oil, then top with leeks. Season to taste with salt.

Arrange cheese over leeks. Lightly crush some or all of the peppercorns and sprinkle over leeks. Scatter walnuts over top. Bake 20 minutes until crust is crisp and golden. Makes 4 servings.

Sausage & Beer Pizza

1 recipe Pan Pizza Dough, shaped and
    ready for topping, page 14

Topping:
1 tablespoon vegetable oil
1/2 teaspoon caraway seeds, if desired
3 tablespoons butter
1 onion, sliced
1 recipe Cheese Topping, page 35, using
    2/3 cup lager instead of milk and 1
    tablespoon German mustard instead
    of dry mustard
8 ounces smoked pork sausage, in one
    piece
1 tablespoon chopped fresh parsley
Tomato slices and chopped parsley, to
    garnish

Preheat oven to 425F (220C). Brush
dough with oil. Sprinkle with caraway
seeds, if desired. Melt butter in a small
saucepan. Add onion; cook 5 minutes
until soft.

Spoon onion mixture over dough.
Spoon Cheese Topping over onion
mixture. Slice sausage into 1/2-inch
slices. Arrange on pizza. Sprinkle with 1
tablespoon parsley; bake 20 minutes
until crust is golden. Garnish with
tomato slices and chopped parsley.
Makes 4 servings.

Sour Cream Caviar Pizzas

**1 recipe Traditional Pizza Dough, made
up to end of step 2, pages 10 and 11**
1 tablespoon vegetable oil

To Serve:
Dairy sour cream or plain yogurt
Caviar, lumpfish or salmon roe
Lemon slices
Chopped fresh chives
Quails' eggs, if desired, hard-cooked

Punch down dough and knead briefly.
Divide into 20 pieces. Roll out each on a
lightly floured surface to a 3-inch circle.
Cover with a towel and let rise slightly.

Preheat oven to 425F (220C). Grease 2
baking sheets. Arrange pizzas on baking sheets and brush with oil. Bake 15
minutes until golden.

Serve warm, topped with sour cream or
yogurt, caviar, lumpfish or salmon roe,
lemon, chives and sliced hard-cooked
eggs, if desired. Makes 6 servings.

Greek Sesame Pizza

1 recipe Traditional Pizza Dough, shaped and ready for topping, pages 10 and 11
1 tablespoon vegetable oil
1/2 teaspoon dried leaf oregano

Topping:
1-1/2 (10-oz.) packages frozen chopped spinach, thawed
2 tablespoons vegetable oil
1 bunch green onions, finely chopped
1 garlic clove, crushed
4 ounces feta cheese, crumbled
1 cup cottage cheese
Salt and pepper
1 egg, beaten
1 tablespoon sesame seeds
Feta cheese, finely sliced and cucumber and olives, to garnish

Preheat oven to 425F (220C). Brush dough with oil and sprinkle with oregano.

Make the topping. Squeeze spinach well to remove excess water. In a medium saucepan, heat oil. Add onions and garlic. Cook, stirring, 2 minutes. Add spinach, crumbled feta cheese and cottage cheese; stir well. Season to taste with salt and pepper.

Stir in beaten egg, then spread mixture over dough. Sprinkle with sesame seeds. Bake 20 minutes until filling is set and crust is crisp and golden. Garnish with sliced cheese, cucumber and olives. Makes 4 servings.

Middle Eastern Pizza

1 recipe Whole-Wheat Pizza Dough,
    shaped and ready for topping, pages
    10 and 11

Topping:
1 pound lean ground beef
1 tablespoon olive oil
1 onion, finely chopped
1 garlic clove, crushed
1 teaspoon ground allspice
1 teaspoon ground cumin
Salt and pepper
2 tablespoons tomato paste
2/3 cup beef stock
1/2 cup dried apricots, chopped finely
2 tablespoons chopped cilantro
Juice of 1 lemon or lime
2 tablespoons pine nuts
1 tablespoon sesame seeds
Lime slices and cilantro sprigs to garnish

To Serve:
Plain yogurt

Preheat oven to 425F (220C). In a medium saucepan, cook beef with the olive oil, onion and garlic until brown, stirring occasionally to break up meat. Drain off fat.

Stir in the allspice, cumin, salt and pepper to taste, tomato paste and stock. Cover and cook 10 minutes, stirring occasionally.

Stir the chopped apricots, chopped cilantro, lemon or lime juice and pine nuts into the meat mixture. Spoon mixture over dough; sprinkle with sesame seeds. Bake 20 minutes until the crust is golden.

Garnish with lime slices and cilantro. Serve at once with yogurt. Makes 4 to 6 servings.

Pizza with Clams

1 recipe Whole-Wheat Pizza Dough,
   shaped and ready for topping, pages
   10 and 11

Topping:
1 pound clams in the shell or 1 (14-oz.)
   can clams
3 tablespoons olive oil
1 recipe Tomato Topping, page 19
Salt and pepper
Few drops hot pepper sauce
2 tablespoons chopped fresh parsley

Preheat oven to 425F (220C). If using clams in the shell, wash well and place in a saucepan with 1 tablespoon oil. Cover and cook over low heat until all the shells open. Discard any that do not open. Remove from heat; strain pan juices into a bowl. Reserve. Remove clams from their shells, reserving a few intact for garnishing. Place shelled clams in reserved juice.

Spread Tomato Topping over dough. Drizzle with remaining oil. Season to taste with salt and pepper and hot pepper sauce and 1 tablespoon chopped parsley. Bake 20 minutes until crust is crisp and golden. Spoon the shelled clams (or canned clams) and a little clam juice over pizza. Arrange reserved clams in shells on top. Sprinkle with remaining chopped parsley. Makes 4 servings.

Mexican Chile Pizza

1 recipe Cornmeal Pizza Dough, made up
   to end of step 2, pages 10 and 11

Topping:
1 pound lean ground beef
1 onion, chopped
1 garlic clove, crushed
Salt and pepper
1 teaspoon ground cumin
1 teaspoon chile powder
2 teaspoons tomato paste
1 (15-oz.) can kidney beans, drained
3 tomatoes, chopped
1 (7-oz.) can whole-kernel corn, drained
1 green bell pepper, chopped
4 to 6 green onions, chopped
1/2 cup (2 oz.) shredded Cheddar cheese

Guacamole:
2 ripe avocados
Juice of 1 lemon
Salt and pepper
3 green onions
Few drops hot pepper sauce

Preheat oven to 425F (220C). Grease a
14" x 10" jellyroll pan. Punch down
dough; knead briefly and place in center of pan. Press out to sides; pinch up
edges to create a rim.

In a medium saucepan, cook beef, onion and garlic until meat browns, stirring to break up meat. Drain off fat.
Season with salt and pepper. Add spices
and tomato paste. Cook 10 minutes.

Rinse and mash kidney beans. Spread
beans over dough. Spoon meat mixture
on top.

Arrange tomatoes, corn and bell pepper and onions on top of pizza as shown
in photo. Sprinkle with cheese. Bake 20
minutes until crust is golden. Make
guacamole by mixing all ingredients in
a blender until smooth. Serve with pizza. Makes 6 to 8 servings.

Curry Pizza

1 recipe Traditional Pizza Dough, shaped
and ready for topping, pages 10 and
11

Topping:
8 ounces potatoes, cooked
2 tablespoons vegetable oil
1 onion, finely chopped
2/3 cup frozen peas, thawed
1-inch piece gingerroot, peeled, grated
1 small green chile, seeded, chopped
1 tablespoon chopped cilantro
1/2 teaspoon ground cumin
1/2 teaspoon ground coriander
2 tablespoons water
1/2 teaspoon garam masala
Salt and pepper
2 tablespoons lemon juice
1 tablespoon sesame seeds

To Serve:
Plain yogurt and onion salad

Make the topping. Cut potatoes into
small cubes. Heat oil in a medium
saucepan. Add onion; cook, stirring 5
minutes. Add potatoes, peas, gingerroot, chile, coriander, water and garam
masala. Cook, stirring, for 5 minutes,
adding more water if mixture becomes
too dry. Season to taste with salt and
pepper; add lemon juice. Let stand for
about 20 minutes.

Preheat oven to 425F (220C). Spread
mixture over the dough, sprinkle with
sesame seeds, then bake in the oven 20
minutes until the crust is crisp and
golden. Serve with yogurt and onion
salad. Makes 4 servings.

Pissaladière

1 recipe Traditional Pizza Dough, shaped
  and ready for topping, pages 10 and
  11

Topping:
1 (16-oz.) can tomatoes
1 onion, chopped
1 garlic clove, crushed
2 tablespoons olive oil
1 tablespoon chopped fresh parsley
2 teaspoons chopped fresh thyme or 1
  teaspoon dried thyme
1 tablespoon tomato paste
1 egg
1/2 cup (2 oz.) shredded Gruyère cheese
Salt and pepper
1 (2-oz.) can anchovy fillets
Ripe olives

Make the topping. Drain tomatoes,
reserving juice. Finely chop tomatoes.
In a saucepan, heat chopped tomatoes
and their juice, onion, garlic, 1 tablespoon oil, parsley, thyme and tomato
paste together. Bring to a boil. Reduce
heat; simmer 30 minutes. Cool slightly.

Preheat oven to 425F (220C). Brush
dough with remaining oil.

Beat egg and stir into tomato mixture
with cheese. Spread over dough. Season to taste with salt and pepper. Drain
and cut anchovy fillets in thin strips.
Arrange in a lattice over pizza. Place
olives in centers of lattice. Bake 20 minutes until crust is crisp and golden.
Makes 4 servings.

Spanish Pizza

1 recipe Traditional Pizza Dough, shaped and ready for topping, pages 10 and 11

Topping:
3 skinned, boneless chicken breasts, cooked
1 tablespoon olive oil
1 onion, chopped
2 bacon slices, chopped
1-1/4 cups long-grain rice
1/2 cup dry white wine
1/2 cup chicken stock
Salt and pepper
1 red bell pepper, chopped
4 ounces chorizo or garlic sausage, sliced
4 tomatoes, seeded, chopped
Few strands saffron, if desired
Parsley and chopped bell pepper, to garnish

Make the topping. Cut the chicken into cubes and set aside. In a medium saucepan, heat oil; add the onion and bacon and fry 5 minutes. Add rice, wine, and stock. Season with salt and pepper. Bring to a boil, cover and cook 5 minutes.

Stir in chopped bell pepper, chorizo or garlic sausage, tomatoes and saffron, if desired. Reduce heat, then simmer 12 to 15 minutes until rice is tender and most of the liquid has reduced. Stir in chicken.

Meanwhile, preheat oven to 425F (220C). Spoon topping on top of the dough, then bake 20 minutes. Garnish with parsley and bell pepper. Makes 6 servings.

Swiss Cheese Pizza

1 recipe Traditional Pizza Dough, shaped and ready for topping, pages 10 and 11
1 tablespoon vegetable oil

Topping:
1 garlic clove, chopped
1-1/2 cups (6 oz.) Cheddar cheese
1-1/2 cups (6 oz.) shredded Gruyère cheese
2 tablespoons kirsch
Freshly grated nutmeg
Pepper
Pimento strips and oregano sprigs, to garnish

Preheat oven to 425F (220C). Sprinkle dough with garlic and shredded cheese. Sprinkle with kirsch, nutmeg and pepper. Bake 20 minutes until crust is crisp and golden.

Garnish the pizza with pimento and oregano. Makes 6 to 8 servings.

Variation: Substitute Emmentaler cheese for the Gruyère cheese, if preferred.

Dim Sum Pizza

1 recipe Traditional Pizza Dough, made up to end of step 2, pages 10 and 11

Filling:
2 tablespoons vegetable oil
8 ounces ground pork
1 bunch green onions, chopped
8 ounces peeled shrimp, thawed if frozen
4 ounces mushrooms, finely chopped
1 tablespoon black bean sauce

To Serve:
Soy sauce
Green onion brushes and carrot flowers

Punch down dough and knead briefly. Divide into 12 equal pieces. Roll out each on a lightly floured surface to a 3-inch circle. Cover with a towel, while preparing filling.

In a medium saucepan, heat oil. Add pork and onions; cook 4 minutes, stirring. Remove from heat, stir in shrimp, mushrooms and sauce. Place 1 tablespoon of filling in the center of a circle of dough. Dampen edges with water, gather together in the center and pinch together. Repeat with remaining circle and filling.

Line trays of a tiered, bamboo steamer with waxed paper. Arrange dim sum on paper and steam over boiling water 30 minutes until firm. Garnish with green onion brushes and carrot flowers. Serve hot with soy sauce for dipping. Makes 6 servings.

Mushroom Calzone

1 recipe Traditional Pizza Dough, made
to end of step 2, pages 10 and 11

Filling:
1 pound mushrooms, sliced
2 tablespoons olive oil
1 garlic clove, sliced
Salt and pepper
1/2 teaspoon dried leaf oregano
8 ounces ricotta cheese
2 tablespoons freshly grated Parmesan
cheese
Beaten egg, to glaze
Grated Parmesan cheese and oregano
sprigs, to garnish

Make the filling. In a medium sauce-pan, heat oil. Add mushrooms and garlic; cook 3 to 4 minutes. Remove with a slotted spoon and place in a bowl. Season to taste with salt and pepper; add oregano. Mix in ricotta cheese and 2 tablespoons Parmesan cheese.

Preheat oven to 425F (220C). Grease 2 baking sheets. Divide dough into 2 equal pieces. Roll out each piece on a lightly floured surface to a 10-inch cir-cle. Brush lightly with oil.

Divide filling between the 2 dough pieces, confining it to one half of each circle. Dampen edges with water, then fold dough over to enclose filling and seal well by pressing with a fork. Trans-fer to baking sheets, brush with beaten egg and make 2 or 3 air holes with a sharp knife. Bake 20 minutes until golden. Garnish with grated Parmesan cheese and oregano sprigs. Makes 4 to 6 servings.

Leek & Onion Calzone

1 recipe Traditional Pizza Dough, made
   to end of step 2, pages 10 and 11

Filling:
3 tablespoons olive oil
2 small leeks, sliced
2 onions, sliced
1 large Spanish onion, sliced
1/2 cup dry white wine
1/2 cup half and half
Salt and pepper
Freshly grated nutmeg
4 ounces stuffed olives, chopped
1 tablespoon olive oil
Leek, onion and olive halves, to garnish

In a medium saucepan, heat 3 tablespoons oil over low heat. Add leeks and onions; cook 10 minutes until soft. Increase heat, add wine and cook until almost dry.

Reduce heat; add half and half. Season to taste with salt, pepper and nutmeg. Cook 2 to 3 minutes until creamy. Remove from heat, stir in chopped olives and set aside.

Preheat oven to 425F (220C). Grease 2 baking sheets. Divide dough into 2 equal pieces. Roll out each piece on a lightly floured surface to a 10-inch circle. Brush lightly with 1 tablespoon oil.

Divide filling between the 2 dough pieces, confining it to one half of each circle. Dampen edges with water, then fold dough over to enclose filling and seal well by pressing with a fork. Transfer to baking sheets, brush with beaten egg and make 2 or 3 air holes with a sharp knife. Bake 20 minutes until golden. Garnish with leek, onion and olive slices. Makes 4 to 6 servings.

Chicken Liver Calzone

1 recipe Traditional Pizza Dough, made
    to end of step 2, pages 10 and 11

Filling:
1/4 cup butter
1 pound chicken livers, trimmed
6 bacon slices, chopped
1 tablespoon chopped fresh sage
1-1/2 pounds fresh spinach, trimmed
Salt and pepper
Lemon juice
Freshly grated nutmeg
Beaten egg, to glaze
Sage leaves, to garnish

Make the filling. In a medium saucepan, melt butter. Add livers; cook
quickly until brown but still pink on the
inside. Remove with slotted spoon and
serve.

Add bacon to saucepan; cook until
crisp. Remove with slotted spoon and
add to livers with chopped sage. Add
spinach to saucepan. Cover and cook
until wilted. Drain well, then chop
coarsely. Season to taste with salt and
pepper, lemon juice and nutmeg.

Preheat oven to 425 (220C). Grease 2
baking sheets. Divide dough into 2
equal pieces. Roll out both pieces on a
lightly floured surface to 10-inch circles. Brush lightly with oil.

Divide filling between the 2 dough
pieces, confining it to one half of each
circle. Dampen edges with water, then
fold dough over to enclose filling and
seal well by pressing with a fork. Transfer to baking sheets, brush with beaten
egg and make 2 or 3 air holes with a
sharp knife. Bake 20 minutes until
golden. Makes 4 to 6 servings.

Broccoli Calzone

1 recipe Pan Pizza Dough, made up to
    end of step 1, page 14
1 teaspoon dried dill weed
1 tablespoon olive oil

Filling:
12 ounces broccoli
2 cups (8 oz.) shredded Cheddar cheese
Salt and pepper
Beaten egg, to glaze
Chopped fresh dill, to garnish

In a medium saucepan of boiling water, blanch broccoli 2 minutes. Drain and refresh with cold water. Drain again. Chop coarsely.

Preheat oven to 425F (220C). Grease 2 baking sheets. Knead dough with dill weed until evenly distributed. Divide into 2 equal pieces. Roll out each piece on a lightly floured surface to a 10-inch circle. Brush lightly with oil.

Divide broccoli between the 2 dough pieces, confining it to one half of each circle. Sprinkle with two-thirds of the cheese and season with salt and pepper. Dampen edges with water, fold dough over to enclose filling and seal well by pressing with a fork. Transfer to baking sheets, brush with beaten egg and sprinkle with remaining cheese. Make 2 or 3 air holes with a sharp knife. Bake 20 minutes until golden. Garnish with fresh dill. Makes 4 to 6 servings.

Watercress Pizza Rolls

1 recipe Pan Pizza Dough, made up to
end of step 1, page 14

Filling:
2 tablespoons butter
1 onion, finely chopped
3 bunches watercress, finely chopped
8 ounces cottage cheese
3 tablespoons grated Parmesan cheese
1 tablespoon lemon juice
1 egg, beaten
Salt and pepper
Watercress sprigs, to garnish

Make the filling. In a medium sauce-pan, melt butter. Add onion; cook 5 minutes until soft. Add chopped water-cress and cook 3 minutes. Remove from heat, stir in cottage cheese, 2 table-spoons Parmesan cheese, lemon juice and egg. Season to taste with salt and pepper. Cool and chill until firm.

Grease a baking sheet. Roll out dough on a lightly floured surface to a 14" x 10" rectangle.

Spread filling evenly over dough leav-ing a small border on all sides. Roll up from one long side to make a firm roll. Seal edges well. Cut into 8 to 10 slices and arrange on greased baking sheet. Cover with plastic wrap and let rise for about 30 minutes.

Meanwhile, preheat oven to 425F (220C). Sprinkle with remaining 1 tablespoon Parmesan cheese. Bake 20 minutes until crisp and golden. Gar-nish with watercress sprigs. Makes 4 to 6 servings.

Pizza Piperade

**1 recipe Cornmeal Pizza Dough made up
to end of step 2, pages 10 and 11**

Topping:
6 eggs
Salt and pepper
1 orange bell pepper, halved
1 yellow bell pepper, halved
2 large or 4 small green onions
1 tablespoon olive oil
2 tablespoons chopped fresh parsley
**Yellow bell pepper rings and parsley
sprigs, to garnish**

Preheat oven to 425F (220C). Grease a
deep 10-inch pizza pan. Punch down
dough and knead briefly on a lightly
floured surface. Place dough in center
of pan, press out to side.

Beat eggs together in a medium bowl.
Season with salt and pepper to taste. Set
aside.

Slice bell peppers into strips; cut onions
into 1-inch pieces. Heat oil in a medium
saucepan, add peppers and onions and
cook 3 minutes, stirring constantly.
Spoon over dough. Pour egg mixture
over bell peppers. Sprinkle with
chopped parsley. Bake 20 minutes until
the egg mixture is set and golden. Garnish with bell pepper rings and parsley
sprigs. Makes 4 servings.

Pizza Ring

1 recipe Traditional Pizza Dough, made
  up to end of step 2, pages 10 and 11
1/2 cup (1-1/2 oz.) freshly grated Parmesan cheese
Salt and pepper

Filling:
2-1/2 ounces pepper salami, sliced
1-1/2 ounces smoked cheese
2-1/2 ounces mozzarella cheese
1-1/2 ounces Gruyère cheese
4 slices processed Cheddar cheese
2 hard-cooked eggs
1 tablespoon olive oil
Lettuce leaves and cherry tomatoes, to
  garnish

Grease a 9-inch ring pan. Punch down
dough, then knead dough with Parmesan cheese and salt and pepper to taste.
Roll out on a lightly floured surface to a
14" x 10" rectangle.

Chop salami and all the cheese into
small pieces. Mix together.

Sprinkle cheese mixture over dough,
leaving a narrow border on all sides.
Halve eggs and cut each half into 3
pieces. Arrange in lines from top to bottom across the length of dough. Roll up
from one long side and seal edges well.

Coil into a circle and seal ends together.
Fit into greased ring pan. Cover with
plastic wrap and let rise 1 hour until
dough is just below top of tin. Brush
with oil.

Preheat oven to 425F (220C). Bake 45
minutes until golden. Serve cold. Garnish with lettuce leaves and cherry
tomatoes. Makes 6 servings.

Salmon Calzoncelli

1 recipe Traditional Pizza Dough, made up to end of step 2, pages 10 and 11

Topping:
4 ounces cream cheese, softened
8 ounces thinly sliced smoked salmon
Pepper
Juice of 1/2 lemon
Lemon slices and chives, to garnish

Preheat oven to 425F (220C). Grease 2 baking sheets. Punch down dough and knead briefly. Roll out dough on a lightly floured surface to 1/8 inch thick. Using a 3-inch cutter, cut out as many circles as possible. Keep covered with a towel while re-rolling dough and cutting out more to make a total of 10 to 15.

In a bowl, mix cream cheese and smoked salmon, pepper and lemon juice. Place 1 teaspoon of mixture on one half of each circle. Dampen edges with water, fold over to enclose filling and seal well by pressing with a fork. Transfer to baking sheets and bake 10 to 15 minutes until golden. Garnish with lemon slices and chives. Serve hot or cold. Makes 10 to 15 servings.

Ham & Salami Calzoncelli

1 recipe Traditional Pizza Dough, made up to end of step 2, pages 10 and 11

Filling:
2 ounces sliced ham
2 ounces sliced salami
2 ounces mozzarella cheese
2 tablespoons chopped fresh parsley
1 tablespoon freshly grated Parmesan cheese
1 egg, beaten
Salt and pepper
Cress sprouts and radish slices, to garnish

Preheat oven to 425F (220C). Grease 2 baking sheets. Punch down dough and knead briefly. Roll out and cut dough as for Salmon Calzoncelli, page 89.

Chop ham and salami very finely. Place in a medium bowl. Shred mozzarella cheese. Add shredded cheese, parsley and parmesan cheese to ham mixture. Stir in egg and season to taste with salt and pepper. Mix thoroughly.

Place 1 teaspoon of the mixture on one half of each circle. Dampen edge with water, then fold over to enclose filling and seal well by pressing with a fork. Transfer to baking sheets and bake 15 minutes until golden. Garnish with cress sprouts and radish slices. Serve hot or cold. Makes 10 to 15 servings.

Variation: Chop 3 ounces mushrooms finely and mix with 6 tablespoons Tomato Topping, page 19, and 1 tablespoon freshly grated Parmesan cheese. Use as the filling.

Leafy Green Calzone

1 recipe Traditional Pizza Dough, made up to end of step 2, pages 10 and 11

Filling:
1 pound Swiss chard
3 tablespoons olive oil
2 onions, chopped
1 (16-oz.) can tomatoes, drained, chopped
2 garlic cloves
1/2 teaspoon dried leaf oregano
Salt and pepper
Beaten egg, to glaze
Tomato slices and marjoram sprigs, to garnish

Trim and discard hard stalks from Swiss chard. Wash well and cook in a large saucepan (with just the water that clings to the leaves) 10 minutes until tender. Drain well and chop finely.

Heat 2 tablespoons oil in a medium saucepan. Add onions; cook 4 minutes until soft. Add tomatoes, garlic and oregano; season to taste with salt and pepper. Cook 20 minutes until thick.

Preheat oven to 425F (220C). Grease 2 baking sheets. Punch down dough and knead briefly. Divide dough into 2 equal pieces. Roll out each piece on a lightly floured surface to a 10-inch circle. Lightly brush with remaining oil.

Mix tomato mixture with the cooked greens. Divide between the 2 dough pieces, confining mixture to one half of each circle. Dampen edges with water. Fold dough over to cover filling and seal well by pressing with a fork. Place on baking sheets, brush with beaten egg and make 2 or 3 air holes with a sharp knife. Bake 20 minutes until golden. Garnish with tomato and marjoram. Serve hot. Makes 4 servings.

Country Calzone

1 recipe Traditional Pizza Dough, made
   up to end of step 2, pages 10 and 11
2 tablespoons olive oil
Mushroom slices and thyme sprigs, to
   garnish

Filling:
1 pound Italian sausages
10 ounces goat's cheese, such as Chèvre
4 ounces mushrooms, sliced
6 to 8 dried tomatoes in oil, see Note
2 dried red chiles, crushed
Beaten egg, to glaze

Preheat oven to 425F (220C). Grease 2 baking sheets. Punch down dough and knead briefly. Divide dough into 2 equal pieces. Roll out each on a lightly floured surface to a 10-inch circle. Brush lightly with oil.

Remove skin from sausages and discard. Cook sausage in a medium skillet, stirring to break up meat. Sprinkle over circles of dough, confining it to one half of circle. Chop cheese coarsely and sprinkle over sausage. Cut dried tomatoes into pieces. Sprinkle tomato pieces, mushrooms and crushed chiles over sausage and cheese.

Fold dough over to enclose filling, dampen edges with water and seal with a fork. Transfer to baking sheets, brush with beaten egg and make 2 or 3 air holes with a sharp knife. Bake 20 minutes until golden. Garnish with mushrooms and thyme. Makes 4 servings.

Note: Dried tomatoes in oil are available from gourmet food shops.

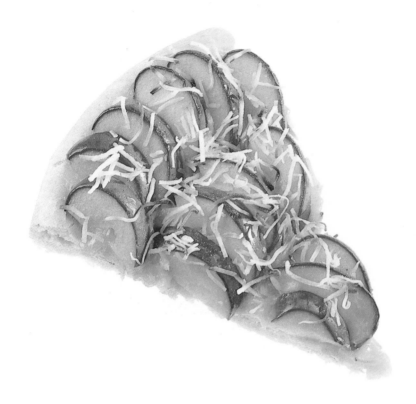

Plum Pizza

1 recipe Deep Pan Pizza Dough, made up to end of Step 1, see page 14

Custard Topping:
7 teaspoons cornstarch
4-1/2 teaspoons sugar
1-1/4 cups milk
Few drops vanilla extract
Few drops yellow food coloring, if desired
1-1/2 pounds plums, halved, pitted
2 tablespoons shredded coconut

To Serve:
Whipped cream

Preheat oven to 425F (220C). Grease a deep pizza pan. Place dough in center, press to edge with your knuckles, then cover and let rise until halfway up the pan.

Meanwhile, make topping. In a bowl, blend cornstarch and sugar with a little of the milk until smooth. Heat remaining milk until nearly boiling. Stir into cornstarch mixture, then return to pan. Bring to a boil, stirring until thickened. Remove from heat, stir in vanilla and yellow food coloring, if desired. Let cool a little.

Slice plum halves into sections. Spoon custard on top of dough. Arrange plum slices on top and sprinkle with coconut. Bake 20 minutes. Serve hot or cold with cream. Makes 4 to 6 servings.

Choc-Truffle Pizza

1 recipe Pizza Dough, pages 10 and 11

Topping:
1 recipe Custard Topping, page 93
3 ounces baking chocolate, melted
8 ounces sponge cake crumbs
1 tablespoon apricot jam
3 ounces white chocolate, melted
1/2 cup finely chopped almonds
White chocolate curls, to decorate

Preheat oven to 425F (220C). Bake dough 20 minutes until golden. Cool.

Meanwhile, make topping. In a bowl, combine custard and melted dark chocolate. Chill until firm.

Make truffles: combine cake crumbs, jam and white chocolate in a bowl until a stiff paste is formed. Divide mixture into small balls and roll in the chopped almonds to coat.

To assemble pizza, spread chocolate-flavored custard on top of baked crust and arrange truffles around the edge. Sprinkle with white chocolate curls. Makes 6 servings.

Raspberry Mallow Pizza

1 recipe Crumble Pizza Dough, made up
   to end of step 3, page 15

Topping:
3 tablespoons raspberry jam
1 pound raspberries
6 ounces marshmallows
Few raspberries and raspberry leaves to
   decorate, if desired

Preheat oven to 425F (220C). Bake pizza dough 5 minutes. Remove from
oven, reduce temperature to 350F
(175C).

In a small bowl, beat jam until soft.
Spread over baked crust. Top with
raspberries. Arrange marshmallows
over the raspberries. Bake 15 to 20 minutes until marshmallows are soft. Cool
before serving. Decorate with raspberries and raspberry leaves, if desired.
Makes 6 to 8 servings.

Tropical Pizza

1 recipe Traditional Pizza Dough, shaped and ready for topping, pages 10 and 11

Topping:
8 ounces fresh dates
4 ounces cream cheese, softened
1 small pineapple
2 kiwifruit

Preheat oven to 425F (220C). Prick dough with a fork, then bake 20 minutes until golden. Cool.

Meanwhile, halve and pit dates. Reserve a few for decoration, then chop the remainder and put in a bowl with the cream cheese. Mix well, then set aside.

Cut top and bottom from pineapple, then cut off skin. Halve pineapple, slice thinly and cut out hard central core. Peel kiwifruit; slice thinly.

Spread cream cheese mixture over baked crust. Arrange slices of pineapple and kiwifruit on top. Decorate with reserved date halves. Cover and refrigerate until ready to serve. Makes 6 servings.

Berry Streusel Pizza

1 recipe Traditional Pizza Dough, shaped and ready for topping, pages 10 and 11

Topping:
1 cup self-rising flour
1/3 cup sugar
1/3 cup butter
1 teaspoon ground cinnamon
2 tablespoons water
1 recipe Custard Topping, see page 93
1 (1-lb.) can gooseberries, drained

To Serve:
Whipped cream

Preheat oven to 425F (220C). Prick dough with a fork and bake 20 minutes until golden. Cool slightly.

In a medium bowl, mix flour and sugar; cut in butter until mixture resembles bread crumbs. Stir in cinnamon and water; mix with a fork until lumpy.

Spoon custard on top of baked crust, top with gooseberries, then sprinkle crumble topping over gooseberries. Bake 10 to 15 minutes until light golden. Serve hot with whipped cream. Makes 6 servings.

Cherry & Almond Pizza

1 recipe Traditional Pizza Dough, made
up to end of step 2, pages 10 and 11
2 tablespoons ground almonds

Topping:
2 egg whites
3/4 cup ground almonds
1/3 cup sugar
Few drops almond extract
8 ounces Morello cherries in juice
1/2 cup sliced almonds
4 tablespoons Morello cherry jam
Powdered sugar for dusting
Whipped cream, to decorate

Preheat oven to 425F (220C). Punch
down dough and knead dough with 2
tablespoons ground almonds.

In a bowl, lightly whisk egg whites. Stir
in ground almonds, sugar and almond
extract. Spread over dough.

Drain cherries, reserving juice. Spoon
over almond mixture, reserving a few
for decoration. Sprinkle with sliced
almonds; bake 20 minutes until crust is
crisp and golden.

Meanwhile, in a saucepan, heat reserved juice and jam until syrupy. Dust
cooked pizza with powdered sugar and
decorate with whipped cream and reserved cherries. Serve the sauce sepa-
rately. Makes 6 servings.

Apple Pie Pizza

**1 recipe Crumble Pizza Dough, made up
to end of step 3, page 15**

Topping:
**3 tablespoons apple or pear butter
2 tablespoons apple juice or water
3 Granny Smith apples, peeled, cored
2 tablespoons raisins
1/2 cup chopped walnuts
1/3 cup packed brown sugar
1 teaspoon ground cinnamon
4 ounces marzipan**

To Serve:
Apple slices and whipped cream

Preheat oven to 425F (220C). Bake dough 10 minutes. Remove from oven and reduce temperature to 350F (175C).

Mix apple or pear butter with apple juice or water to form a soft paste. Spread over baked crust. Slice apples thinly. Place in a medium bowl with the raisins, walnuts, sugar and cinnamon. Mix well. Spoon over baked crust and level surface. Grate marzipan and sprinkle over surface. Bake 25 to 30 minutes. Serve with apple slices and whipped cream. Makes 6 servings.

Lemon Meringue Pizza

1 recipe Traditional Pizza Dough, shaped and ready for topping, pages 10 and 11

Topping:
3 tablespoons cornstarch
1-1/4 cups sugar
1/3 cup water
2 eggs, separated
Juice and grated peel of 2 lemons
Star fruit slices and lemon balm, to garnish

Preheat oven to 425F (220C). Prick dough with a fork. Bake 20 minutes until golden. Cool slightly. Reduce oven temperature to 350F (175C).

Make topping. In a medium saucepan, combine cornstarch and 1 cup sugar. In a small bowl, combine water and egg yolk. Stir egg yolk mixture into sugar mixture. Cook, stirring, over medium heat until bubbly and thickened. Stir in lemon juice and peel. Spread over baked crust.

In a large bowl, whisk egg white until soft peaks form. Whisk in remaining sugar gradually. Pipe or spoon on top of lemon mixture to cover filling completely. Bake 10 minutes until meringue is golden. Decorate with slices of star fruit and lemon balm leaves. Makes 6 servings.

Christmas Calzone

1 recipe Pan Pizza Dough, made up to
end of step 1, page 14

Filling:
1/2 cup unsalted butter, softened
3/4 cup powdered sugar, sifted
2/3 cup packed brown sugar
1 tablespoon milk
1 tablespoon brandy
6 tablespoons mincemeat
Powdered sugar for dusting

Preheat oven to 425F (220C). Grease 2
baking sheets. Divide dough into 2
equal pieces. Roll out each piece to a
10-inch circle.

Make the filling. In a bowl, beat butter
and sugars together. Gradually stir in
milk and brandy until mixture is light
and fluffy.

Place 1 tablespoon brandy butter and 3
tablespoons mincemeat to one side of
each circle of dough. Brush edges with
water, fold over and seal edges firmly.
Transfer to baking sheets and bake 20
minutes until golden.

Dust with powdered sugar. Serve warm
with remaining brandy butter. Makes 4
to 6 servings.

Pear & Ginger Pizza

1 recipe Pan Pizza Dough, shaped and
  ready for topping, page 14

Topping:
4 pears, peeled, cored
3 tablespoons apple or pear butter
1/2 cup chopped walnuts
2 tablespoons chopped crystallized ginger
2 tablespoons butter, melted
Crystallized ginger and angelica, to decorate

To Serve:
Whipped cream

Preheat oven to 425F (220C). Chop 2
pears and put in a medium bowl with
the apple or pear butter, walnuts and
ginger. Mix well, then spread over the
dough.

Halve remaining pears. With a sharp
knife, slice each half from the round
end to the point without cutting
through. Fan out the section and arrange on top of the pizza. Brush with
melted butter. Bake 20 minutes. Decorate with crystallized ginger and angelica and serve with whipped cream.
Makes 4 to 6 servings.

Banana-Maple Syrup Pizza

1 recipe Traditional Pizza Dough, shaped and ready for topping, pages 10 and 11

Topping:
2 tablespoons butter, melted
4 bananas
2 to 3 tablespoons maple syrup
Chopped walnuts and whipped cream, to decorate

Preheat oven to 425F (220C). Brush dough with a little melted butter.

In a bowl, mash 2 bananas with maple syrup. Spread over dough. Slice remaining bananas. Arrange over mashed bananas. Brush with remaining melted butter. Bake 20 minutes until crust is crisp and brown.

Pipe whipped cream around edge of pizza. Decorate with walnuts. Makes 4 to 6 servings.

Orange Liqueur Pizza

1 recipe Pan Pizza Dough, shaped and ready for topping, page 14

Topping:
2 tablespoons butter, melted
3 oranges
2 tablespoons orange liqueur
2 tablespoons orange marmalade
2 tablespoons brown sugar
Whipped cream and mint sprigs, to decorate

Preheat oven to 425F (220C). Brush dough with melted butter.

Using a zester, remove strips of orange peel; set aside for decoration. Peel oranges thinly with a sharp knife or potato peeler. Cut off white pith and discard. Slice oranges thinly. Arrange over dough.

In a pan, heat liqueur, marmalade and sugar until syrupy. Spoon over oranges and bake 20 minutes. Meanwhile, blanch peel strips in boiling water 2 to 3 minutes. Drain and cool. Decorate pizza with orange peel strips, cream and mint. Makes 6 servings.

Berry Cheesecake Pizza

1 recipe Crumble Pizza Dough, made to
  end of step 3, page 15

Topping:
1-1/2 pints strawberries
12 ounces Neûfchatel cheese
1/2 cup milk
Grated peel of 1/2 orange
1/4 cup orange juice
2 tablespoons honey
1 egg, beaten
2 tablespoons red currant jelly
Whipped cream and strawberry leaves, to
  decorate

Preheat oven to 425F (220C). Bake
dough 15 minutes. Meanwhile, hull
and chop half the strawberries. In a
medium bowl, blend Neûfchatel cheese
with milk, orange peel, orange juice,
honey and egg.

Spoon chopped strawberries over
baked crust. Spoon cheese mixture
over strawberries and smooth top. Bake
35 to 40 minutes until set. Switch off
oven, open door and allow cheesecake
to cool gradually.

In a saucepan, heat red currant jelly
until melted. Arrange reserved
strawberries on top of cheesecake.
Brush with melted jelly. Decorate with
whipped cream. Makes 6 servings.

Panettone

2 (1/4-oz.) packages active dried yeast
1/3 cup warm water (110F, 45C)
1/3 cup sugar
4 egg yolks
1 teaspoon vanilla extract
Grated peel of 1 lemon
3 cups bread flour
1/2 teaspoon salt
1/3 cup butter, softened
1/3 cup chopped candied peel
2 tablespoons dark raisins
2 tablespoons golden raisins
1/4 cup butter, melted

In a small bowl, combine yeast, 1 teaspoon sugar and the water; leave until frothy.

In a large bowl, combine remaining sugar, egg yolks, vanilla and lemon peel. Stir in yeast mixture. Mix flour with salt. Gradually add two-thirds flour to yeast mixture to form a sticky dough.

Divide softened butter into 3 equal pieces. Add one piece at a time, kneading until mixture is heavy and stringy. Add remaining flour; mix well. Knead on a lightly floured surface until firm and buttery, but not sticky. Place in a bowl. Cover with plastic wrap; let rise in a warm place 1-1/2 hours until doubled.

Preheat oven to 400F (205C). Well grease a charlotte pan. Knead peel and raisins into dough. Place in pan, cover and let rise to just below top of pan.

Brush with melted butter; bake 10 minutes. Reduce temperature to 350F (175C). Brush again with butter; bake 30 to 40 minutes until browned. Brush with more butter after 15 minutes. Cool. Makes 10 to 12 servings.

Grape Bread

**1 recipe Pizza Dough, made up to end of
  step 1, page 14**
2 tablespoons fine sugar

Filling:
12 ounces red seedless grapes
1/4 cup fine sugar

To Serve:
Sugar and whipped cream

Preheat oven to 425F (220C). Grease a deep 10-inch pizza pan or cake pan.

Spread grapes on a baking sheet and bake 10 minutes. Meanwhile, punch down dough and knead with 2 tablespoons sugar. Divide into 2 equal pieces. Roll each piece to a 10-inch circle. Remove grapes from oven; turn off oven.

Place one dough circle in greased pan. Brush surface with water and spoon over half the grapes. Sprinkle with half the remaining sugar. Lay second piece of dough on top and press gently with fingertips to seal dough around grapes and make small pockets.

Spoon remaining grapes over the surface and sprinkle with remaining sugar. Cover with plastic wrap and let rise in a warm place 1-1/2 hours. Preheat oven to 400F (205C). Bake 20 to 25 minutes until golden. Cool, then dust with extra sugar and serve with whipped cream. Makes 6 servings.

Walnut Bread

1 recipe Whole-Wheat Pizza Dough,
    made up to end of step 2, pages 10
    and 11
1-1/4 cups (5 oz.) chopped walnuts
Vegetable oil

Grease a baking sheet. Punch down dough and knead in walnuts. Flatten to a 10-inch round loaf shape. Place on greased baking sheet. Cover with plastic wrap and let rise in a warm place 1 to 1-1/2 hours until doubled in size.

Preheat oven to 375F (190C). Brush dough with oil. With a sharp knife, make 2 or 3 slashes across the top. Bake 20 to 25 minutes until bottom sounds hollow when tapped. Cool on a wire rack. Serve sliced and buttered with cheese or plain with soup or pasta. Makes 5 to 8 servings.

Pizza Loaf

1 recipe Pan Pizza Dough, made to end
   of step 1, page 14
3 ounces sliced salami, chopped
3 green onions, finely chopped
1 tablespoon chopped fresh herbs

Topping:
Melted butter for brushing
4 slices processed Cheddar cheese

Tomato & Basil Butter:
3/4 cup butter, softened
1 tablespoon tomato paste
2 tablespoons finely chopped basil
1 teaspoon lemon juice

Grease an 8" x 4" loaf pan. Punch down dough and knead dough with salami, green onions and herbs. Shape into a loaf. Cover with plastic wrap and let rise in a warm place until dough almost reaches top of pan.

Preheat oven to 375F (190C). Brush loaf with melted butter. Bake 25 to 30 minutes until loaf sounds hollow when bottom is tapped. Turn out of pan and place on a baking sheet. Slice cheese into strips and place in a lattice design over top. Return to oven 3 to 4 minutes to soften cheese a little. Cool.

Make Tomato & Basil Butter. In a small bowl, beat butter with tomato paste, basil and lemon juice. Spoon into a serving dish and cover and refrigerate until required. Slice Pizza Loaf and serve with Tomato & Basil Butter. Makes 6 servings.

Bread Sticks

**1 recipe Traditional Pizza Dough, made
  up to end of step 2, pages 10 and 11**
**Sesame or poppy seeds, or cracked
  wheat, to sprinkle**

To Serve:
Slices of prosciutto, if desired

Preheat oven to 400F (200C). Grease
several baking sheets.

Punch down dough and knead briefly.
Divide dough into approximately 18
equal pieces and roll each piece to an
8-inch length. Arrange on greased baking sheets and brush with water.

Leave plain or sprinkle with sesame or
poppy seeds, or cracked wheat, if desired. Bake 15 to 20 minutes until crisp
and golden. Cool before serving plain
or wrapped with slices of prosciutto, if
desired, to serve as a cocktail snack.
Makes about 18.

Polenta Bread

1-1/3 cups coarse ground cornmeal
1 cup all-purpose flour
1-1/4 teaspoons salt
1/4 teaspoon pepper
3 tablespoons olive oil
1 cup lukewarm water

To Serve:
Salad

Preheat oven to 425F (220C). Grease a 12-inch pizza pan. In a medium bowl, mix together the cornmeal, flour, salt and pepper. In a small bowl, whisk together 2 tablespoons oil and water. Stir into the flour mixture with a fork to form a grainy paste.

Place in center of pan and press to edges with knuckles. Prick with a fork and brush with remaining oil. Bake 20 minutes until golden. Serve the bread warm with salad. Makes 4 to 6 servings.

Focaccia

1 recipe Traditional Pizza Dough, made
  up to end of step 2, pages 10 and 11
1 teaspoon crushed dried rosemary
About 18 pitted green olives
Coarse sea salt, to sprinkle
Rosemary sprigs, to garnish

Preheat oven to 425F (220C). Grease a 12-inch pizza pan.

Punch down dough and knead dough with crushed rosemary. Place dough in center of pan and press to edges with your knuckles. Prick all over with a fork. Press olives into dough. Brush with water and sprinkle with sea salt. Bake 20 minutes until crisp and golden. Garnish with rosemary. Makes 4 to 6 servings.

Variations: Omit green olives and knead chopped ripe olives into dough with rosemary.

Or knead 1/2 cup freshly grated Parmesan cheese into dough and season to taste with a little pepper. In both cases, prick dough with a fork, brush with water and, if desired, sprinkle with sea salt before cooking.

Piadina

2-1/2 cups bread flour
1-1/4 teaspoons salt
1/2 teaspoon baking powder
1/3 cup milk
1/3 cup water
3 tablespoons olive oil

To Serve:
Salami, cheese and salad

In a medium bowl, mix flour, salt and baking powder. In a measuring cup, combine milk and water. Add oil and a little of the water and milk mixture to flour mixture. Stir with a fork and gradually add more liquid until it has all been incorporated. Mix to form a soft dough.

Turn onto a lightly floured surface and knead until smooth. Cover and rest for 15 minutes. Divide dough into 12 equal pieces. Roll each piece out to a 3-inch circle.

Heat a heavy skillet or griddle until a drop of water flicked on the surface bounces and evaporates. Place 2 to 3 circles in skillet and cook 30 seconds. Flip over and continue cooking.

Turn each circle 2 or 3 times until sides are speckled with brown. Place on a wire rack while cooking remaining circles. Serve warm with salami, cheese and salad. Makes 12.

Pizza Margherita, page 19

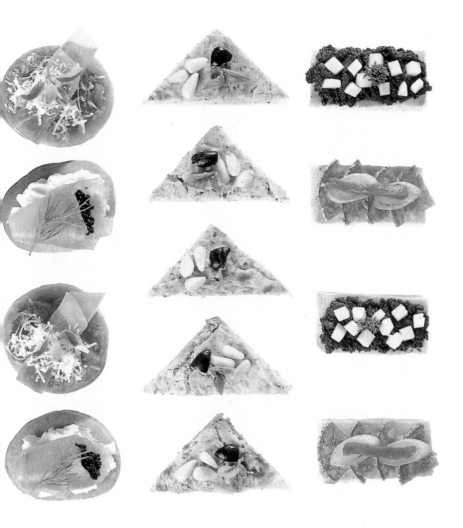

Left: Pizza Canapés, page 50; Ham & Tomato Bites, page 44
Center: Pesto Pizzelle, page 45
Right: Pizza Canapés, page 50; Mozzolive Bites, page 53

Mexican Chile Pizza, page 76

Pizza Ring, page 88

Orange Liqueur Pizza, page 104

Clockwise from top:
Walnut Bread, page 108; Polenta Bread, page 111;
Bread Sticks, page 110; Piadina, page 113; Focaccia, page 112;
Grape Bread, page 107; Panettone, page 106;
Pizza Loaf, page 109

INDEX